Theatrical FX Makeup

Theatrical FX Makeup

David Sartor

John Pivovarnick

Heinemann
Portsmouth, NH

Heinemann

A division of Reed Elsevier Inc.
361 Hanover Street
Portsmouth, NH 03801–3912
www.heinemanndrama.com

Offices and agents throughout the world

The author and publisher wish to thank those who have generously given permission to reprint borrowed material:

Figure 2.2 reprinted with permission from *Forensic Pathology* by Dominick J. DiMaio and Vincent J. M. DiMaio and *Techniques of Crime Scene Investigation*, 5th Edition, by Barry A. J. Fisher. Copyright © 1993 by CRC Press, Boca Raton, Florida.

Library of Congress Cataloging-in-Publication Data
Sartor, David.
   Theatrical FX makeup / David Sartor, John Pivovarnick.
       p. cm.
   ISBN 0-325-00238-X (pbk.)
      1. Theatrical makeup.   I. Pivovarnick, John.   II. Title.
PN2068 S27 2001
792'.027—dc21   2001024127

Editor: Lisa A. Barnett
Production: Lynne Reed
CD production: Wunderkind Studios
Cover design: Night & Day Design
Manufacturing: Steve Bernier

Printed in the United States of America on acid-free paper
05 04 03 02 01 RRD 1 2 3 4 5

I'd like to dedicate this book to the Monkey Man, Eric Nicholas Durkin, who always lets his uncle turn him into the coolest things for Halloween. I hope you never outgrow it.

Love, Uncle
—John Pivovarnick

This book is dedicated to my mother, Helen Wassel Lancia, for all of her love and support. I can't wait until your book comes out. And to my big brother Chad Toth, you're one of the best men I know. Thanks for your guidance and friendship.

Love, David

Contents

Contents

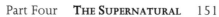

Acknowledgments

No one writes a book alone—particularly this one. Many talented and generous people gave of their time, their experience, and their *stuff* to help us. With much gratitude, we would like to acknowledge their contributions.

In the stuff department, we are indebted to the following people and companies for providing advice and materials:

- Pat Saito-Lewe and Ben Nye, Inc., for providing all of the Ben Nye products you'll see used throughout the book. We don't feel guilty for plugging them, because we would have used their product line even if they hadn't given it to us

- Andre and Jenny Di Mino of ADM Tronics, Inc., for supplying us with Pros-Aide, another product we would have purchased if it had not been graciously offered. As promised: *Pros-Aide adhesive is provided and developed by ADM Tronics, Northvale, NJ (201) 767-6040. Pros-Aide is a trademark of ADM Tronics*

- John Patterson at LensQuest, for cutting us a deal on the special-effects contact lenses

- Michael Davy of Michael Davy Film and TV Makeup, for providing his Collodacolor colored collodion, Sweat Stop, and Adhesive Blending Paste

In the time department, we are eternally indebted to

- Colleen McGovern, video diva, for videotaping most of our makeup sessions and occasionally photographing them as well. She also subjected herself to wearing one of our creations

- John Yeomans, for modeling, for photographing, and for lending us reference materials from his father's medical, dental, and forensic pathology library

We are also pathetically grateful to the kind folks who modeled for us, submitting their faces to all manner of abuse. They are, in order of appearance in the book: Helen Lancia, John Smolskis, Linda Eisen, John McGurl, Karen Razler, Susan E. Walton, John Yeomans, Matt Harchick, Sierra Lancia, Ashley Lancia, John Thomas, Colleen McGovern, Phoebe Sharp, James McGurl, and Michael McGurl.

Some of these folks traveled great distances, through all sorts of weather, only to find themselves with mushy soap in their hair, contacts in their eyes, and all manner of stuff glued to their faces. That's what you call a real friend.

Introduction

Welcome to the World of Special FX Makeup

I don't care who you are or what your background is; at some point in your life you've seen a makeup effect onstage, in a movie, or on television and wondered, "How'd they *do* that?"

That's how we started with effects makeup—as did probably everyone else in the field. Experimentation as teenagers led to more and more interest (okay, *obsession*), which led to more elaborate Halloween preparations, as well as more disgusting pranks played on our friends.

Some of us are devoted enough to continue on, going on to study effects makeup in school—if we're lucky enough to find a school that offers it. Otherwise, we teach ourselves.

The problem with teaching yourself how to do effects is that many tricks of the trade, particularly the gross-out ones appropriate for torturing friends, are held as closely guarded secrets. There are some books available on effects makeup, but many of them are more autobiographical than informational. That's very frustrating to an eager teenager or even a professional makeup artist who is suddenly called upon to do some effects work.

That's the reasoning behind this book. We wanted to write the effects makeup book *we* wish we'd had when we started out: one with basic, how-to information and lots of leeway for personal experimentation and exploration.

While the book is called *Theatrical FX Makeup*, the techniques shown also apply to television and film. The designs just require a little more finesse and subtlety to read well in those media.

How the Book Is Organized

The book is broken down into four sections.

Part One, "Getting Ready," deals with preparation and planning. It covers the basic tools and supplies required to execute the designs discussed in the rest of the book, as well as giving advice on research and documentation, explaining how to set up a work area, and establishing some key concepts to keep in mind as you're creating designs on your own.

Part Two, "Simple Effects," gives you an easy, hands-on way to introduce yourself to some of the basic techniques that will be used extensively in the more elaborate makeup designs of later chapters. It gives you an introduction to core painting techniques, a primer on working with three-dimensional materials, and possibly more than you ever wanted to know about making and using stage blood.

Part Three, "Full-Face Effects," presents nearly a dozen full-face designs with step-by-step instructions and photographs. The designs build off the tools and techniques of the first two sections and are limited to human (and perhaps slightly inhuman) creations.

Part Four, "The Supernatural," goes a little further outside the box, to present more elaborate, less human designs.

All along the way, the designs are accompanied by suggested uses, variations, and ways to tinker with the designs to adapt them to your own needs and interests. You'll also find a few appendices at the end of the book that provide helpful information, resources, and a place to take your own notes while reading the book or experimenting with makeup.

Using This Book

We recommend at least reading the first two sections before you dive in to the full-tilt designs. Depending on your level of experience, you may want to play around with some of the techniques covered in Part Two before you move on to the more complex designs in the later sections.

When you feel comfortable with the basic techniques, feel free to jump around however the spirit moves you. You know what you want or need to get out of this book better than we do.

We've tried to be thorough in cross-referencing relevant material (recipes and techniques) for each of the designs, so even if you're skipping around, you should have no trouble finding the information you need.

When you begin adapting these techniques for your own use, keep in mind that these designs were created and executed to illustrate the process in a tiny studio, without the benefit of a lit stage on which to test them. Depending on the size of your theater, you will have to adjust the makeup to accommodate the distance between the actor and the audience.

More distance gives you a lot more leeway in terms of masking seams and requires less subtlety in the application of the makeup. As shown here, these effects are probably not *exaggerated* enough for a theater with a twenty- to thirty-foot separation between the stage and the front row and not *subtle* enough for an intimate black box theater or for film and video work.

The short version: *test* your variations on these designs in the space in which they will be seen *before* you trot them in front of an audience or a camera.

What This Book Isn't

Just so you know upfront, preferably in the bookstore before you've shelled out your hard-earned cash, this is *not* everything you'll need to know about effects makeup. This is square one—and maybe square two.

In writing this, we've assumed a certain level of experience in makeup design and application. If you're coming to this fresh, with no grounding in the basics of makeup for stage, screen, or video, you might want to pick up a companion book to give you that foundation (pardon the pun). There are a number of good ones available.

Additionally, we've limited the effects to those that are easily achieved without a huge investment in materials and equipment. These are tried-and-true effects that don't require life casts, molding equipment, or ovens in which to cure appliances. They are also core techniques that carry over to *any* effects makeup.

While foam latex and other appliances are de rigueur, especially in Hollywood and on television, the design, creation, finishing, and application of such appliances would be a book unto itself. In the best of all possible worlds, this would be the first book in a series of three or four titles that would run the gamut of effects makeup techniques and technology.

Technical Information

For the propeller heads in the audience, principal photography for the book was done with a Sony Mavica MVC-91 digital camera. Supplemental photos were taken with a Canon AE-1 35mm SLR camera on Fuji 800-speed film. Video segments were shot using a Canon ES-80 8mm camcorder; we *wanted* a Canon XL-1 digital camcorder, but hey, a budget's a budget.

Part 1

...ting Ready

..e, of the makeup artist's work is accomplished
..'s face. That work may include attending design
..:ctor and artistic staff, doing research, roughing
..akeup to see if desired effects can be achieved by

..iing is everything.
..lp you plan ahead, by explaining the tools and
supplies you'll find essential and those you may find nice but not necessary, as well
as outlining suggested strategies for setting up a work area, compiling research material, and anticipating some of the challenges associated with using effects makeup
onstage.

1
Tools and Supplies

*E*very job has its basic set of tools, whether it's a secretary's word processor, a sculptor's chisel and mallet, or an engineer's calculator. The special-effects makeup artist is no different. In fact, effects makeup can call on the tools of several trades and several artistic disciplines.

> In case you missed it on the acknowledgments page, you should know that the Ben Nye Company graciously outfitted us with its products for use in the writing of this book. You should also know that, if it hadn't been so generous, we would have purchased them anyway—and in some cases, we did.

The basis of every makeup will be the standard range of theatrical makeup that should be in every makeup artist's basic kit.

Makeup Essentials

It is difficult to categorize the essential makeup supplies in anything other than very general terms. The number and colors of the various foundations, highlights, shadows, and rouges will vary widely depending on the skin tones of the actors on whom they will be applied.

New makeup artists and new theater companies would find it economically unfeasible to stock up on *every* shade and every variation just in case. Ben Nye produces a line of more than one hundred shades of foundation alone.

Basic Makeup Supplies

The essential supplies necessary for any makeup artist are given in the following list. The product numbers given are for the Ben Nye products that we used, unless otherwise noted. However, makeup artists get notoriously attached to certain products and manufacturers. You, of course, are free to use whatever products you like.

- ⮷ Assorted foundation colors in a range of shades suitable to your typical cast of actors. Use whatever type of foundation you prefer—cake, crème, or crème stick. We used Nye's Tan No. 1 cake foundation (PC-9) and Old Age crème foundation (PP-5)
- ⮷ Creme Shadow color wheel (SK-3), or assorted shadow colors
- ⮷ Creme Highlight color wheel (SK-2), or assorted highlight colors
- ⮷ Clown White (CW-2)
- ⮷ Creme Cover All blemish wheel (SK-1), which functions as a cover stick
- ⮷ Mellow Yellow (MY-2, normal), which is a beard and blemish coverup and color neutralizer
- ⮷ Generic liquid foundation in appropriate shades, both oil- and water-based; we used Max Factor Ivory
- ⮷ Black and brown eyeliner, cake or liquid
- ⮷ Mascara (Max Factor)
- ⮷ Eye shadow in a neutral range (taupe, brown), plus any shades you prefer
- ⮷ Powdered rouge (Misty Pink, DR-6)
- ⮷ Neutral Set colorless face powder (MP-2)
- ⮷ Plain talcum powder

These will give you the ability to do a variety of straight, street, and simple effects. However, when you move into some of the more complex and esoteric effects, you'll need some additional supplies.

FX Makeup Supplies

This is a listing of *all* of the products we used to create the effects shown throughout the rest of this book. In the real world, it would be impractical to run out and buy them all. You should supplement your basic makeup kit with effects additions on an as-needed basis. To that end, each makeup chapter includes a listing of the products used for that particular makeup, so you can get only those items you need for the makeup you want to duplicate.

Foundations and Color Wheels

- ➲ Cake foundation, *Blithe Spirit* (PC-8)
- ➲ Creme F/X Bruises wheel (CK-1)
- ➲ Creme F/X Cuts and Bruises wheel (CK-3)
- ➲ Creme F/X Burns and Blisters wheel (CK-5)
- ➲ Creme F/X Severe Exposure wheel (CK-9)
- ➲ Creme F/X Age Stipple wheel (CK-7)
- ➲ Bronzing Body Tint (BT-2)
- ➲ Mehron greasepaint set, flesh tones
- ➲ Mehron greasepaint set, primary colors

FX Accessories

- ➲ Crepe hair

    Dark Auburn (WH-7)

    Light Brown (WH-9)

    Medium Brown (WH-10)

    Dark Brown (WH-12)

    Black (WH-22)

- ➲ Mortician's wax (NW-4), also known as nose and scar wax or nose putty, but it's actually the stuff morticians use
- ➲ Vaseline, to simplify handling the mortician's wax
- ➲ K-Y Jelly
- ➲ Kryolan rigid collodion
- ➲ Michael Davy's Collodacolor colored collodion (red)
- ➲ Stage Blood (SB-7), 32 ounces
- ➲ Thick Blood (TB-1)
- ➲ Gel Blood (GE-1)
- ➲ Fresh Scab (TS-1)
- ➲ Flesh Effect Gel (GE-3)
- ➲ Temporary hair color sprays (brown, silver, black, and white); any brand will do.
- ➲ Prosthetic Molding Paste (Michael Davy)
- ➲ Latex eye bags (Burman Industries)

⊃ Latex ear tips (Burman Industries)

⊃ Latex bald cap (Burman Industries)

⊃ Single-ply toilet tissue

⊃ Facial tissue

⊃ Assorted food coloring

⊃ Unflavored gelatin (Knox)

⊃ Nye's temporary tooth colors (Nicotine, Black, and Decay or Zombie Rot)

⊃ Special-effects contact lenses (completely optional, due to the expense, if you opt for them, however, you'll also need accessories such as lens cases in which to store your lenses, as well as wetting and cleaning solutions)

Adhesives and Solvents   We used these products to attach and remove various dimensional effects throughout our designs.

⊃ Spirit gum

⊃ Liquid latex

⊃ Pros-Aide (ADM Tronics)

⊃ Isopropyl alcohol

⊃ Bond Off! (BR-2)

Tools

Every craftsperson has tools specific to his or her craft. For the effects makeup artist, there are the tools you would probably expect—brushes, sponges, and the like—and some you probably would never expect. This is the list of the tools we used while executing the makeup designs for this book.

⊃ Makeup brushes—a large assortment of small, medium, and large sizes with fine, flat, and angled tips. We used a No. 2 custom round (RS-2), a No. 2 flat (FB-2), a No. 7 flat (FB-7), a No. 12 flat (FB-12), a No. 4 angled shadow brush (AB-4), and a rouge brush (RB-2)

⊃ Inexpensive (i.e., disposable) paint brushes for some of the more tenacious adhesives and chemicals

⊃ Cotton swabs

⊃ Makeup sponges of the wedge variety

⊃ Stipple sponge (NS-1)

- Friendly Plastic, for teeth, horns, and other effects
- Artificial teeth, available from dental supply houses
- Moist towelettes
- Paper towels
- Bar towels for cleanup
- Bath towels to protect clothes and other surfaces
- Hair brush
- Comb
- Barrettes
- Bobby pins
- Hair bands, clips, or scrunchies for getting longer hair up and out of the way
- Scissors, various sizes
- Razor blade or precision knife, such as an X-Acto knife
- Disposable razors and shaving cream

Miscellaneous Items

These are items you wouldn't normally expect to find in a run-of-the-mill makeup kit; however, they are very helpful and necessary for one or more of the designs presented here. The manufacturers and suppliers for the more esoteric items that you won't find in your local hardware, craft, or art supply store are included in the suppliers index in Appendix B, Suppliers and Distributors.

- Permanent markers, assorted colors
- Design markers (alcohol-based), assorted colors
- White feathers
- Plastic bird mask
- Black spray paint, high-gloss enamel
- Superglue
- Hot-melt glue sticks and glue gun
- Surgical tape
- Small-gauge aquarium air hose
- Saucepan

7

➲ Wooden or plastic spoon

➲ Measuring cups

➲ Hot plate or stove

➲ One- and two-inch paint brushes

➲ Dremel or similar multifunctional rotary tool

You may already have some of these items or you may be able to borrow them. For the rest of the items listed, you may or may not want to acquire them until you decide which effects you want to try on your own.

You may also want to set yourself the challenge of accomplishing these effects with whatever tools and supplies you already have, and that's a practical, real-world exercise if ever there were one.

2

Basic Skills

Venturing into the arena of special-effects makeup builds upon the skills you've already developed as a makeup artist. Effects makeup, however, may take you places you've never dreamed of going. When was the last time you found yourself trying to talk your way into a hospital morgue with a camera under your arm? (This past September, here. Thanks for asking.)

By its nature, effects makeup forces you to study and analyze things that most people would prefer not to think about. Cuts and wounds, blood and pus, and how do you get a five-foot-tall actor to look like an eight-foot-tall demon?

Imagination is key.

So is knowledge.

This chapter includes some practical suggestions on how to draw on your imaginative resources and how to expand your store of knowledge, and it covers some practical matters that face the effects makeup artist on a daily basis.

Learn by Playing

You can exercise your imagination and add to your knowledge base simply by playing around with your makeup.

One of the key factors in designing an effective, lasting makeup is knowing the strengths and limitations of the materials at your disposal. The easiest way to learn that is to try them out.

If you find yourself looking at a makeup presented here—or on television or in a movie—and wondering, "What would happen if I did this . . . ?" try it on yourself or a friend.

If you wonder whether liquid latex can support the weight of, say, a hard-boiled egg when attached to an actor's face, get out a pot and boil an egg. How large of a mortician's wax hematoma do you need for a fork to stand up in it?

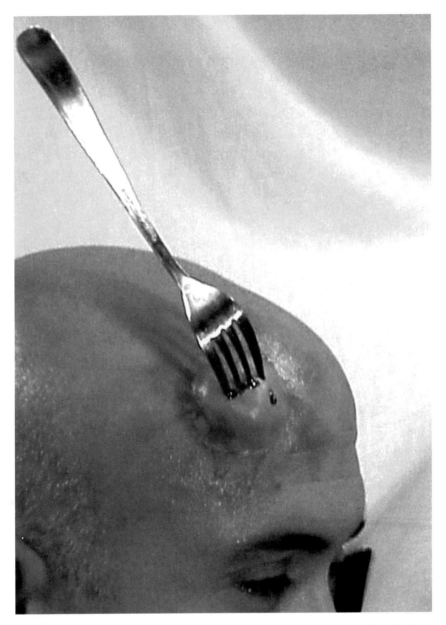

Figure 2.1   How large of a mortician's wax hematoma do you need for a fork to stand up in it? Apparently, this large. (Model: John Pivovarnick)

The experiments that work will give you a new trick you can keep up your sleeve until you need it. Those that don't will save you time later on.

You don't want to have to spend a lot of time experimenting under the pressure of an opening-night deadline. Learn and play and experiment when the pressure is off. Let your friends know you're always looking for victims (for some reason, they're always the most willing during the last week of October). Borrow an actor. Work on your own face.

While you're playing, write down your process—not only what works but what doesn't. Take some pictures. Videotape the experiment. When you're done playing, make a note of your findings. You never know when that information will come in handy.

Documentation and Research

Another related set of tools that is useful for the effects makeup artist is research and, as mentioned earlier, documentation.

Documentation is easy: When you find a cool new use of liquid latex, write it down. Keep a journal or a sketchbook of notes. You don't have to be anal-retentive about it, but *don't* rely on your memory, and don't entrust your information to random scraps of paper. Keep it all together.

If you *want* to be anal-retentive about it, go ahead. Build a database on your computer. Cross-reference and cross-index it all, and be able to query it seven ways to Sunday—whatever works for you. The important thing is that you can find the information you want, when it's needed.

Research is also key.

Most makeup artists keep some sort of photo morgue. It may be a box or a scrapbook of photographs of interesting faces, clippings from newspapers and magazines, or photocopies of illustrations from historical works for period reference. The effects makeup artist needs all of these and then some. What if you need to create an Elizabethan zombie sometime or need to design the reptiles for Edward Albee's *Seascape?*

Pretty much anything is fair game for an effects morgue, from pictures of animals and creatures, to photocopies from Uncle Fester's *Big Book of Scabs*, to videotapes of movies and television shows with inspiring effects makeup. You can see a sample from a couple of the books* we used as research in Figure 2.2 They were actually borrowed from a friend, John Yeomans (our model in Chapter 10). His father is a forensic dentist—the doctor they mean when they say, "The victims were identified from their dental records."

Forensic Pathology (by Dominick J. DiMaio and Vincent J. M. DiMaio, CRC Press, 1993) shown in Figure 2.2, and *Techniques of Crime Scene Investigation, 5th edition* (by Barry A. J. Fisher, CRC Press, 1993).   11

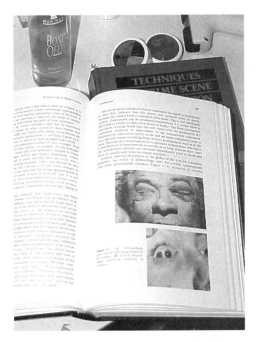

Figure 2.2   Medical reference books and forensic pathology books make excellent research materials for the effects makeup artist.

Some excellent resources for you include

- ◗ Medical book stores—many hours of nauseating fun can be had flipping through books on dermatology, surgical techniques, and forensic pathology

- ◗ Used book stores and college bookstores that carry used books—these offer the same resources as a medical book store, but at a discount

- ◗ Photo-intensive magazines—*National Geographic, Smithsonian,* or any other magazine can provide glossy fuel for your imagination

- ◗ Cable television—the Discovery Channel, the Learning Channel, the History Channel, Animal Planet, A & E, Fox, hey, even E! if you catch a good episode of *Mysteries and Scandals.* Always keep a blank tape in your VCR when you're channel surfing

- ◗ Your local video store—there's nothing like an effects makeup flick to get your mind spinning, take apart Johnny Depp's makeup in *Edward Scissorhands,* or get some *really* god-awful, low-budget, trashy horror movie like *Beware! Children at Play* and figure out where the effects went wrong

➲ The Internet—there's actually a lot of excellent research material out there, if you can winnow through all of the nonsense. The leprosy makeup in Chapter 13 was actually based on photographs found on the Web

➲ The library—your local library probably contains any and all of these resources under one roof, and for *free*

Wherever you find your research materials, build up a reference library of clippings, printouts, and photocopies of the information that may prove useful to you in the future.

> Of course, to get the most out of the Web, you need to know what you're looking for and use a good search engine to track it down. You can start at a search engine like Yahoo! (*www.yahoo.com*) or Lycos (*www.lycos.com*) and see where it leads you. When you find your reference material, you should print out or download a copy of the Web page(s) for your personal reference collection.

Setting Up a Work Area

Not every theater is blessed with an abundance of backstage space. It isn't always possible to have a dedicated green room, much less a full-time makeup room. The key to any makeup area, whether it's nomadic or permanent, is lighting, organization, and comfort.

Lighting

To be effective, you must be able to see at least a rough approximation of what your final makeup will look like when presented onstage; that means you need light, and lots of it.

In a permanent makeup room, a makeup mirror with built-in lights—the classic image of a makeup room—can provide adequate lighting. However, more nomadic, impermanent theaters will have to cobble together a makeup area that is not only efficient but also portable.

Inexpensive, moveable lighting can be as simple as a few swing-arm architect lamps or even the clip-on work lamps available in most hardware stores. They allow a certain level of flexibility, as long as you have enough places to clip them and plug them in, and they can also be gelled to approximate the lighting conditions onstage while you work.

When possible, you can also rely on natural light, which will give you a brutally honest look at your makeup.

Organization

Let's face it: in order to create a makeup effect, you have to be able to find the makeup you need. That means two things: adequate workspace, in the form of a table where you can lay out the materials you'll need, and a safe storage locker in which to keep those materials when not in use.

We'll talk about material storage a little later. For the moment, let's focus on the worktable. It doesn't have to be lavish, but it should provide enough space to lay out your tools and equipment, plus room for your notes, beverages, and whatever else you might want to put there. It should also have a mirror in which both you and the actor may check your work.

In a permanent facility, your worktable can be as large and elaborate a structure as your budget can manage. Traveling makeup artists may have to resort to a folding table or even something like the one shown in Figure 2.3. This is the one we used when creating the designs throughout this book. It's actually an old Brunswick bowling table, rescued from the destruction of a local bowling alley. It's worked out rather well—aside from the slight angle of the tabletop.

Figure 2.3   Almost any table can be jury-rigged into an adequate worktable—even an old bowling table like this.

Comfort

Actors being given a basic stage makeup can sit in any sort of chair with little wear and tear to themselves or to the makeup artist. With an effects makeup, however, the actor may be trapped in that chair for some time, and the makeup artist will spend an equal amount of time bent over the actor applying the effect. That is, literally, an uncomfortable situation all around.

To save both the actor and the makeup artist some discomfort, you should have as comfortable a chair as possible. For a permanent makeup room, an installed makeup chair (like a barber's chair) that can be raised or lowered and has a built-in headrest is ideal—expensive, but ideal. It gives the actor's head adequate support, preventing him from getting neck strain while the makeup is being applied. The adjustable height allows the makeup artist to raise the actor up to a comfortable working level to avoid lower-back strain and pain.

An adjustable office chair with armrests and a high back is a less-expensive substitute that will work well for the actor. It is a little less ideal for the makeup artist, since office chairs tend not to have the range of adjustability to raise the actor to a height that is comfortable for working.

Other niceties that can make both you and your actor comfortable include

- Relaxing music—if you want to be nice, let your actor select the music, and play it softly in the background
- Beverages—have some ice water or soft drinks available. Depending on the makeup, you may need to be sure you have straws, too. It's hard to sip a drink through a few pounds of latex
- Mints or chewing gum—this is as much for your own comfort as the actor's. Some actors are a little lax in the dental hygiene department, and you don't want to smell *that* any longer than necessary. Return the favor, as well. Be sure *your* breath is fresh before you set up shop for the day

> In the "it couldn't hurt" department, one makeup artist I know keeps a bottle of mouthwash, a new, inexpensive toothbrush, and a travel-sized tube of toothpaste in her makeup kit at all times, just in case she, or someone she's working on, is in major need of a little dental hygiene. It couldn't hurt.

Material Handling

There are two main concerns when it comes to handling the specialized materials associated with effects makeup: safety and hygiene.

Safety Issues

Safety is a primary concern—safety for yourself, your actors, and even your theater. Many of the materials used in effects makeup are dangerous in one way or another, and as such, they should be handled cautiously.

The list of materials discussed here is generic at best. Always read the product label for instructions on proper use and any safety warnings. Manufacturers aren't shy about warning you of the dangers of misusing their products.

When in doubt, or when you're working with a new actor, you might want to patch test all of the makeup products you'll be using with him or her. Just apply a small amount of each item to the actor's inner arm, leave it on for an hour or so, and see if the skin reacts.

- ↺ Flammable liquids—many adhesives, solvents, and even some makeup products are alcohol- and/or petroleum-based. They should be used away from open flame, and no smoking should be allowed near them, either

- ↺ Irritants—some makeup products may irritate or burn sensitive tissues like the eyes or nasal passages. Extreme care should always be used around the eyes, nose, and mouth of your actors. Actors with sensitive skin may have an adverse reaction to some of these preparations even when used correctly. If they do, discontinue their use

- ↺ Dangerous vapors—(insert your own "vapor" joke here) besides the flammable/inflammable products, others such as liquid latex have a noxious smell until the liquid cures or sets. In the case of liquid latex, it's ammonia. Hair sprays, collodion, and other staples of the effects makeup trade are equally smelly. Use with proper ventilation

- ↺ Toxicity—some effects makeup products, while safe for external use, may be poisonous if ingested. The greatest confusion arises in the many varieties of stage blood available: some are flavored and completely edible, others are not

Use common sense when handling makeup products, particularly some of the more esoteric items involved in effects makeup.

Hygiene Issues

Most actors prefer to carry and use their own individual makeup, it saves them time and ensures that no one has handled or used their makeup aside from themselves. That's with good reason. Shared makeup can spread germs and viruses like those that cause colds and cold sores. Additionally, simple cross-contact might bring on a rash or hives on an actor with sensitive skin, just as shaving with someone else's razor can.

Unfortunately, most actors don't schlep around the tools of the effects makeup trade. When applying a makeup effect, there is bound to be some sharing of makeup products, particularly things like stage blood and liquid latex, which come in quart- and even gallon-size bottles.

There are steps you can take to minimize the risk to yourself and your actors when making up several people using the same set of makeup supplies.

- *Work from a palette.* Mix your makeup colors on a palette (a glass plate works well) that you can wash frequently, or clean the surface of the makeup with alcohol between actors (just lightly run over the surface with a cotton ball moistened with alcohol).

- *Wash your hands often.* Most makeup artists tend to use their fingers as a brush or sponge. That's fine, but remember to wash your hands before you begin working on the next actor. Add a fingernail brush to your kit, and use it to scrub the buildup out from under your nails. Those waterless hand-sanitizing products are also good to have around. They won't remove any leftover makeup from your hands, but they will kill any germs you may have picked up on them.

- *Don't reuse sponges.* When you're finished with an actor, dispose of the sponges you've used to apply his or her makeup. Use a fresh set of sponges for your next actor.

- *Clean your brushes.* Good brushes are expensive and therefore not a disposable commodity. Make sure you wash your brushes between actors. Use warm, soapy water, a commercial makeup remover, or a brush-cleaning solution (most makeup companies offer one as part of their product lines). You could even work like a painter, keeping your brushes submerged in a cleaning solution while you work, making sure that they're always clean and dry before you begin using them.

Additionally, you can stick to disposable paper products such as tissues and paper towels for cleaning up. Actors should provide their own towels and washcloths for washing up after a performance. If you dislike the waste of disposable paper products, you can lay in a supply of inexpensive cloth towels (those sold as bar rags at most restaurant supply houses work well); just be sure they're used for only one actor, then laundered before their reuse.

Material Storage

It's just like my mother used to say: when you're through playing with them, it's time to put your toys away. There are two primary concerns with storing your makeup supplies: where they are stored and how.

Preparation for Storage

As you're cleaning up your work area and getting ready to put everything away for the night, there are a few things to check.

Be sure everything is properly sealed. Crème makeup dries out. Alcohol-based products evaporate. Liquid latex and other adhesives turn into big gooey bottles of crud—expensive crud, at that. An improperly closed bottle of spirit gum can leak all over your makeup case, ruining the spirit gum and probably taking several other makeup supplies with it.

When you're packing up, simply get into the habit of testing the lids of your various supplies to make sure that they are properly sealed. Some products, particularly adhesives, tend to clog up at the mouth of the bottle, either giving you a bad seal that could leak or allow the product to dry out or *permanently* sealing the bottle so you can't get it open.

To prevent this, wipe the mouth of the bottle down with a paper towel dampened with a little alcohol or other solvent. It will keep the seal from either extreme— leaking and drying out or never opening again.

When storing your own concoctions—your own special blend of blood or effects gelatin, for example—make sure to keep them in small bottles or jars that seal well. Baby food and small mayonnaise jars work well. Also make sure your concoctions are clearly labeled and dated, so you know what's in the jar and how long it's been sitting on your shelf.

With brushes and other tools, make sure to clean them thoroughly before storing them. It will extend the life of your tools and save you from having to clean them before you begin the next day.

The Storage Unit

Depending on the size of the theater company you're working with, this could be as simple as throwing a few makeup wheels in a shoebox or loading up a secure, wall-mounted storage cabinet.

For our purposes, since putting together the makeup effects for this book has been a fairly moveable feast, we resorted to the four-tiered, wheeled storage cart shown in Figure 2.4. While it lacks the security of a metal storage unit with a lock, it makes up for it by being compact and lightweight and having four different-size trays to accommodate all the various sizes of makeup paraphernalia. As a bonus, it's just the right height to act as a small side table, if you put a cutting board or piece of plywood on top. We purchased it for under twenty dollars at one of those wholesale clubs.

Portability is especially a concern for freelance makeup artists, whose materials stay with them at all times. You might want to have a large makeup storage box at home, then use a smaller, more portable tackle box to carry just the items you'll need with you to work.

Figure 2.4   This wheeled storage unit has the benefits of being lightweight and portable and of accommodating a large variety of different-size materials.

Whatever you use to store your supplies, it should be lockable. Whether the storage unit itself locks or it can be moved into a room that can be locked is up to you. The locking is as much to prevent people from playing with hazardous substances and possibly injuring themselves as it is to keep them from stealing your stuff. This is doubly important for productions that have children in the cast. If your storage unit allows it, you should try to store the more dangerous items on a top shelf, out of reach of youngsters.

Summing Up

Effects makeup is a unique field that demands a lot of multidisciplinary work. It takes all of the skills of a traditional makeup artist and pushes them into new and wondrously strange areas that combine both art and science.

Keep the following basic points in mind when designing and creating innovative makeup effects.

- ⊃ Make use of multidisciplinary research methods and any and all of the resources at your disposal.
- ⊃ Experiment to learn the strengths and weaknesses of your materials and to see what other little tricks you can come up with.
- ⊃ Maintain an archive of both your research and the results of your experimentation for future reference.
- ⊃ Once you've got your research in place, and a project on which to work, setting up and maintaining an efficient work area is essential.
- ⊃ Efficiency and organization is completely subjective; set up and maintain your area in the way that works best for you.
- ⊃ Safety and hygiene considerations, however, are not subjective, and every effort should be made to maintain a clean, hygienic, and safe makeup room.

3
Design
Considerations

Any art form is a process of communication that relies, in part, on the perception and interpretation of its audience. For the sculptor or painter, it's a fairly straightforward process: the artist creates, then the audience views, interprets, and reacts.

Makeup artists, by contrast, have to go through a process of interpretation and negotiation long before their hands ever touch a brush or a pot of makeup.

It begins with the script, someone else's art, which must be interpreted and processed to come up with the design concept. That initial concept then has to be further interpreted and, more often than not, modified by the director, other members of the production design team, and sometimes even the actor on whom the makeup will ultimately be applied.

Once the artistic considerations have been settled, the practical considerations are put to the test: Can the budget support the design? Is the makeup durable? Does it read from the back of the house? Does it work as well on a face as it did on the illustration board?

You can see the design and refinement process in action in the figures presented here, which show the development of the makeup for Chapter 22, "The Creature." The first two sketches, shown in Figure 3.1, show the initial design concept. After meeting and discussing the concept in terms of the needs of the chapter—which in the real world would be in terms of the production—the design was refined and shaped to exploit the features of the model's face (Figure 3.2), most notably, his lack of hair and his willingness to wear a special contact lens to simulate a cataract. The final design rendering is shown in Figure 3.3.

In the best of all possible worlds, there is ample time to research and conceptualize, then to work through the negotiating and refining process: first preproduction

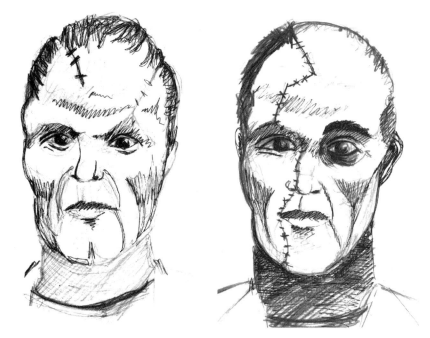

Figure 3.1   Design concepts for our version of Frankenstein's monster.

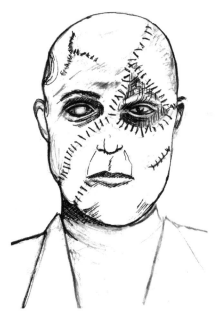

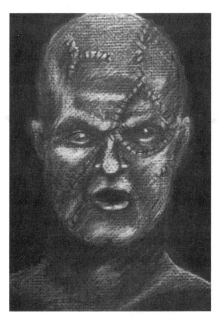

Figure 3.2   The Creature makeup refined.

Figure 3.3   The final design of the Creature makeup for Chapter 22.

meetings would be held to discuss concepts; then preliminary sketches would be presented and refined; then production meetings would be held to further refine and modify the design with a particular actor cast in the role; and finally, technical rehearsals would be conducted to test and further refine the design in the context of the whole production.

However, no one ever claimed this was the best of all possible worlds.

Sometimes work just falls into your lap. You get little or no time to work the process, and you have to rely on your knowledge and experience to help you fly by the seat of your pants. Design sketches may be nothing more than rough doodles on a bar napkin, if any get done at all. The design process is always a function of the amount of time you have, your working relationship with the director (one you've worked with before may not need or want concept sketches from you), and, as always, the production budget.

Regardless of the amount of time you have, you can sidestep some of the more common design pitfalls by keeping a few key concepts in mind: the love/hate relationship between an actor and his makeup; how the actor and other elements can affect the permanence of a makeup; and how lighting can affect the makeup's appearance onstage.

Makeup and the Actor

Some actors view even the most basic makeup as a necessary evil, a way to keep their faces and expressions from getting washed out by distance and powerful lighting. Others view the donning of makeup as an integral part of getting into character and/or as a way of hiding themselves from an audience so they are psychologically free to do whatever the role demands of them.

Effects makeup, because it tends to obscure the actor's real face to some degree, aggravates those who see makeup as a thing to be tolerated. The actors who view makeup as a liberating mask or as a way into a character tend to be more tolerant of the heavier effects makeup.

The psychology of actors and acting would be a book unto itself. Don't try to figure it out; simply be prepared to stick to your guns and deal with the peculiarities of the actors you have to deal with.

Depending on the personality of the actor, the amount of stage time involved, and the complexity of the makeup, there are a couple of factors that need to be weighed when designing a makeup effect: comfort and impairment issues inherent in the makeup.

Comfort

Effects makeup is rarely comfortable to wear. The adhesives may tingle and burn during application and itch during a performance. Whatever is being applied to the actor—whether it's a latex appliance, sculpted putty, or anything else—can weigh on the actor's face; promote sweating, which in turn will affect the permanence of the makeup; and generally irritate the actor and/or his skin.

Removal can also inflict a certain level of discomfort and skin irritation, particularly if the actor is of the rip-and-run school of makeup removal.

Actors with sensitive skin can have pronounced and severe reactions to makeup and adhesives. When auditioning a role that will require extensive makeup, it's a good idea to let the actors know about it in advance so they can warn you of any known allergy conditions. There's nothing like casting an actor for a role only to find out he's allergic to latex during dress rehearsal.

If an actor warns you that she has sensitive skin, it's a good idea to test the makeup by applying a dab of each element—paint, adhesive, and any appliance materials—to the actor's inner arm to see what reaction her skin will have, exactly the same way an allergist would. Depending on the reaction(s), you might have to alter your design or materials to accommodate.

Changing actors is an extreme option—depending on the importance of the makeup to script or the director's interpretation of the script—but it's an option nonetheless. In preproduction for *The Wizard of Oz*, Buddy Ebsen (Barnaby Jones and Uncle Jed on *The Beverly Hillbillies*) had a horrible reaction to the tin woodsman's powdered aluminum makeup that landed him in the hospital under an oxygen tent. That's how Jack Haley wound up with the role.

As a general rule of thumb, you should try to follow the Bauhaus idea of less is more. Design the makeup to get the maximum effect with the minimum amount of makeup.

Making the design as comfortable as possible to wear also helps to ensure that the makeup will go on as designed, especially if the actor is responsible for its application during the run of the show.

Impairment Issues

Some makeup effects can impair an actor's ability to perform in a number of ways:

- Full-face, masklike makeup can affect the actor's ability to speak and to see.
- Some special contact lenses or heavy makeup over and/or around the eyes can limit the actor's ability to see or affect his depth perception.
- Prosthetic teeth can affect the actor's ability to speak.

Vision impairment is especially dangerous. We've all heard stories of performers who have landed in the orchestra pit because they couldn't see where they were going.

When a required effect poses a performance or safety problem to the actor, the best course of action is to give the actor ample time to get used to the impairment. That may mean giving the actor several rehearsals with the full makeup or providing a simulation of the effect that the actor can work with both during rehearsals and on his own.

For example, an effect that covers an actor's eye can be easily simulated by giving him an eye patch to wear during rehearsals. A pair of rehearsal teeth can be supplied to give the actor the chance to get used to working around any prosthetic teeth.

> Depending on the severity of the impairment, it may be necessary to station an assistant in the wings to act as a guide for the actor, particularly during blackouts or fast scene changes and in the darkened conditions backstage.

The Permanence Factor

It's a rule of nature: what goes up must come down. As a corollary, what gets glued must come unglued.

There's nothing more disheartening—or embarrassing—than to have a makeup fall off an actor onstage or in front of the camera. Several factors can affect the permanence of any effects makeup. Some can be anticipated and accommodated; others are beyond the designer's control.

Physicality

A lot of facial movement, whether from speaking or exaggerated expression, can loosen facial appliances. While a sturdy adhesive like Pros-Aide will help, it's still a good idea to avoid, when possible, the use of large appliances around the mouth or to design the appliances in pieces to minimize the amount of flexing to which the appliance is subjected.

Roles that involve stage combat or other strenuous activity can make the actor sweat, which will loosen facial appliances and fade painted effects. Depending on the role and the makeup, it may be necessary to have someone in the wings touch up the makeup as needed between scenes.

Some actors just sweat a lot onstage, whether from the heat of the lights or from performance anxiety. Sweat is destructive to any makeup, but particularly an effects makeup. Whether the actor is playing Mephistopheles himself or third demon from the left, if sweat is a problem, you should just cut to the chase and use Pros-Aide as your adhesive. You can also try applying an antiperspirant to the actor's face—either the run-of-the-mill drugstore variety or a makeup-specific product like Sweat Stop from Michael Davy Film and TV Makeup.

Environmental Factors

Most environmental factors are beyond the control of the makeup artist. The weather is the weather, no matter how much you complain about it, but it can affect your work.

Heat and high humidity can have a debilitating effect on makeup. Both prompt actors to sweat, as discussed earlier. The solution remains the same: stronger adhesives and touching up as necessary.

Additionally, humidity can have an effect on hair, both natural and crepe. For natural hair and wigs, an extra measure of styling may be required to overcome the weather's effects. Gels and/or mousse can be used to tame frizziness while retaining the designed hairstyle.

Humidity can be especially devastating to crepe hair, and particularly the adhesives used to apply it. The traditional crepe hair adhesive, spirit gum, surrenders easily to humidity and sweat. Crepe hair applied directly to the skin will shed, and there isn't a lot you can do about it. Your only recourse is to use prepared beards and mustaches (on backing material) and be ready for constant touchups throughout the performance.

You should, of course, warn your actor when any factor may affect the permanence of his makeup. An actor can be very easily thrown by the feeling that a piece of his face is about to fall off. Forewarned is forearmed, and the actor can mentally prepare for the need for touchups between scenes and can orchestrate ways to subtly reapply the cranky appliance, should it begin to slip midscene.

Lighting and Makeup

Theatrical lighting, at its best, allows all of the production's designers to showcase their work in, pardon the pun, the best possible light. Sometimes, however, the best possible lighting for a scene is not the best lighting for your makeup. This is especially true for effects makeup.

Generally speaking, makeup effects are presented in dramatic or atmospheric lighting; monsters tend to come out at night, witches stir their cauldrons in dim caves during thunderstorms, and ghosts favor candlelight.

A makeup artist with any experience knows the trauma of watching the delicate makeup for a rosy-cheeked child turn into a gray-and-black spotty mess when hit with green light. The problem is that stage lighting adds color to your carefully selected palette of makeup colors. That lovely shade of rose blush you blended will turn gray or black in green light or a bruised shade of purple under blue light.

The problem stems from the fact that, as with paint, color mixing in makeup works from the three primary colors: red, yellow, and blue. In paint, when you mix all of the colors together, you get black. Paint without pigment is white.

In light, the primary colors are red, green, and blue. White light is composed of all the colors. There is no black-colored light—that would be the absence of light.

There is no simple solution to the problem, since the variety and shades of makeup matched with the variety and shades of lighting gel give you an almost infinite assortment of bad color combinations. Table 3.1 shows the nine possible color outcomes when a primary color of light is thrown on a primary color of paint.

There are, however, two solutions that will help you avoid most of the color-mixing pitfalls.

First, you can work with the lighting designer to see what gel colors will be used for the production, especially those for key makeup scenes. If time allows, you can test variations of the makeup under the actual stage lighting conditions, either on the actor(s) in question or on a cooperative volunteer.

This solution will sidestep problems on a case-by-case basis. If you document your findings, you can build up a solid reference manual of makeup and lighting dos and don'ts. Be anal-retentive about this; record your findings by color combinations, but also include makeup and gel information by manufacturer, color name, and color numbers.

Table 3.1   A simple illustration of the effect of colored light on colored makeup.

	Light		
Paint	*Red*	*Green*	*Blue*
Red	Red	Deep Brown	Deep Purple
Yellow	Red-Orange	Yellow-Green	Black
Blue	Black	Blue-Green	Blue

Second, you can educate yourself. Take a course in color theory and a basic introduction to stage lighting. The immediate benefit will be to keep stage lighting from trashing your makeup, but you will also gain useful information that will help you design spectacular effects that require the combination of makeup and light to be successful, for example, a subtle death's head makeup that is undetectable until it's hit with green or blue light.

The research and documentation suggested in the previous chapter coupled with the proactive approach to the design and execution of your makeup suggested in this chapter can make your designs, if not impervious, at least *less susceptible* to whims of fate.

Part 2
Simple Effects

Most people think spectacular, blood-spurting effects when they think of FX makeup, however FX makeup can be as simple and subtle as an unnoticeable application of liver spots on an actor's hand.

Even the most elaborate of effects can be made or broken by the way in which the small details are handled. The devil is, after all, in the details.

This section of the book gives you a basic grounding (or refresher) in core techniques that you will carry with you and use throughout the rest of the book, including paint techniques, basic dimensional effects, and instructions on how to construct some of your own FX accessory pieces. You'll even get a basic primer on blood and other bodily fluids to help lay the groundwork for the full-face effects in later sections.

4
Paint Techniques

The temptation with effects makeup is to discard the tried-and-true methods of makeup in favor of the newest, the latest, the greatest technological advance. In some instances, that's a good thing; many effects chores are made much easier by advances in technology. However, you should never discard basic painting techniques—ever.

Painted effects still play a role in even the most elaborate effects makeup. They provide the finishing touches that bring latex appliances to life, mask our mistakes, and give detail to the makeup that we would never be able to achieve otherwise.

In this chapter you'll get an introduction to (or a refresher on) the basic effects painting techniques—actual brushwork, or spongework, or fingerwork, or whatever your tool of choice may be. Keep in mind that, while we're looking at individual techniques, most makeups use a combination of these techniques to achieve a natural, if not realistic, look. *Natural* and *realistic* are very relative terms when you get into some of these effects, but you know what we mean.

You should always use what works best for you and looks the best in the circumstances in which you find yourself working. A paint effect that works well in a large, proscenium theater might look like hell in an intimate black box, and vice versa. There is, however, a general rule of thumb: the closer the audience—or the camera—is to your work, the less you'll be able to get away with.

A really good makeup can be examined up close, without any seams or brush strokes showing—illusion at its best. Luckily, for most, the audience never gets that close—certainly never as close as we get with some of the illustrative photographs you'll see in this and other chapters.

Basic Techniques

There are a handful of basic techniques that you can combine and modify in any way that suits your needs. These aren't hard-and-fast rules, however; they're simply the starting point. Matisse, Hopper, and Seurat all used the same set of basic painting skills, yet with *very* different results. Painting is not an inappropriate analogy here, since many of these techniques are at the heart of painting, especially scene painting, in which creating an illusion is every bit as important as it is in makeup.

These should be practiced and played with so you can develop your own styles and variations. Keep in mind that many makeup artists have worked long and hard to develop their techniques and keep many of them secret.

We'll discuss the basic techniques in two general groups: *application* (ways of laying paint on the skin) and *blending* (ways to blur, blend, and add subtlety to your applied makeup).

Application Techniques

We're going to describe four main ways of applying paint to skin or prosthetics, shown in Figure 4.1. For the sake of the discussion, and for display in a black-and-white photograph, these are *very simple*. Remember that you can—and should—modify these techniques by layering in multiple colors, applying more or less makeup of different values and intensity, and combining both the application and blending techniques to give you an almost infinite variety of results.

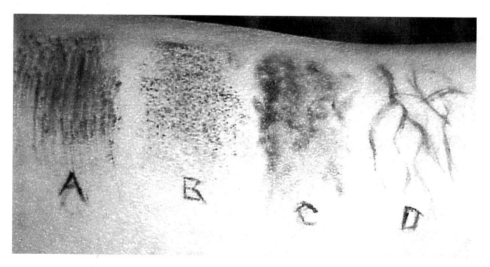

Figure 4.1   Four basic methods for laying paint on skin using a stipple sponge or brush.

In Figure 4.1, you'll see the four techniques, labeled A through D. They are, from left to right,

⮑ Stipple/streak (A)—a technique by which a stipple sponge loaded with paint is dragged quickly across the skin. It's commonly used for scrapes, brush burns, and dirt, but you can use it (or any of these techniques) wherever you need it

⮑ Pouncing (B)—another stipple sponge technique, by which the paint is lightly dabbed on the skin, leaving the imprint of the stipple sponge. The common uses include five-o'clock shadows, broken capillaries, and age spots

> Many makeup artists refer to the pouncing technique as *stippling*, since it is the basic use of the stipple sponge. We've used a nontraditional term to help differentiate between the techniques simply because you can't use the word stipple everywhere without someone getting confused. We've borrowed this term from painting. Once you've mastered the technique, you can call it whatever you want.

⮑ Mottling (C)—a technique by which paint is applied unevenly and blended to show natural discoloration, typically used for bruises and the marbling of corpses

⮑ Veining (D)—a straight brush technique by which paint is applied in veinlike patterns. It's common in painted age effects for wrinkles and varicose veins. It can also be used for postmortem effects. When veining, random portions should be blended more than others, creating the illusion of depth for that subcutaneous look

Again, these techniques are usually used in combination as part of an overall design and, depending on the desired effect, in two or more colors. Once they are applied, they're also blended into the to rest of the makeup using one of the techniques that follow.

Blending Techniques

No matter the sort of makeup you're doing—bloody, decaying zombie or a fashionable street makeup—blending is everything. It softens lines and edges and gives a natural look to whatever effect you're going for.

For very subtle effects, you may want to consider investing in an airbrush. It allows for very fine application of liquid makeup that will stand up to scrutiny even under the zoom lens of a camera. An airbrush is also an excellent tool for finishing large latex appliances; applying makeup with a sponge or brush to an appliance can often feel like you're painting stucco.

To achieve the desired effect, you can blend with your finger, a sponge, a brush, or a cotton swab. For subtler effects, you may want to use a tiny amount of an appropriate solvent, such as water or isopropyl alcohol, to help blend.

You can see the four basic blending techniques demonstrated in Figure 4.2. They are, from left to right,

- ⮑ Gradient blend (E)—a simple one-color gradient blend achieved by laying in an area of color and fading it into the background color. It's used to sculpt and reshape areas

- ⮑ Negative blend (F)—Color is selectively removed from a solid field. The technique lends weight and texture to a mottled surface

- ⮑ Blend and Blur (G)—shows multiple levels of general blending and blurring of the dots of makeup. The first column of dots is untouched, while the others are each more blended and blurred into the flesh

- ⮑ Juxtaposition (H)—laying a light color next to a dark is a core principle of all makeup; think of the highlight and shadow used to draw wrinkles or sculpt a cheekbone. The contrast makes the light line pop, and therefore appear raised, while the dark area recedes. The two-color gradient demonstrates the gradual transition between shadow and light, also used to sculpt and contour

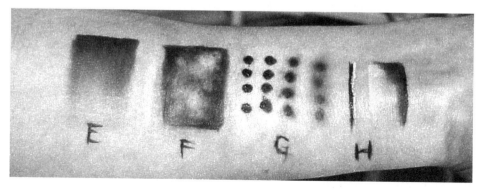

Figure 4.2   Four basic blending techniques, labeled E through H.

Once mastered, these simple techniques can be put to many varied and effective uses, as demonstrated in the following sections. The techniques are quite simple but incredibly flexible and limited only by your imagination and experimentation. That sounds corny as hell, but it's true.

Highlight and Shadow Reference

While practicing your paint techniques on yourself or on a convenient victim, you might also want to brush up on the various highlight and shadow areas of the face.

These highlight and shadow areas come into play whenever you do a basic makeup, but particularly when you age an actor, create the look of a wasting illness, reshape the face with paint, or give life to a zombie or other undead creature.

Figure 4.3 is a handy reference photograph that shows the heavily accented planes and shadows of a face.

You may want to make a photocopy of this page to keep in your work area or in your photo morgue.

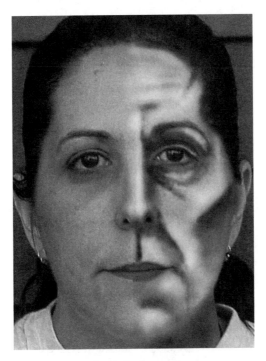

Figure 4.3   A facial shadow reference, graciously worn by Helen Lancia.

Simple Painted Effects

These effects use one or more of the techniques covered earlier. While they are handy effects to know, they also give you a chance to practice the techniques with a definite goal, rather than dabbing makeup all over your arms and face.

Five-O'clock Shadow

Beard stubble (shown in Figure 4.4) is done with the pouncing or stipple technique. Using a stipple sponge, stipple the actor's face with crème color to match his hair or beard color.

To get a natural look, you need to be careful not to overlap too much (dark borderlike areas will form) or too little (creating open, uncovered areas in the beard). When the paint is applied, you need to powder it carefully; otherwise, it will smudge.

Change over to a lighter-brown palette of colors, and smudge and blend to your heart's content, and you have an effective technique for dirt and mud.

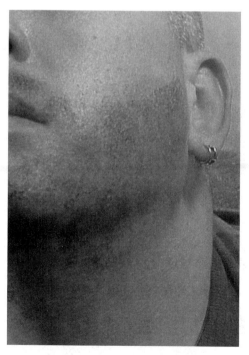

Figure 4.4   Beard stubble is created with a basic stipple technique. (Model: John Pivovarnick)

Bruises

Bruises (shown in Figure 4.5) are done with a combination of mottling and blending in the various shades the body produces when bruised, which are conveniently assembled in bruise wheels by Ben Nye and other makeup companies.

The color palette will change, depending on the age of the bruise. The one shown in Figure 4.5 is relatively recent, with a highlight color toward the center of the primary bruise, blending to a deep purple at the outer extreme.

Abrasions

Abrasions, or road rash, brush burns, scrapes—whatever you want to call them—are created with a simple stipple/streak. A stipple sponge, loaded with thick stage blood or makeup, is quickly swiped over the area to be abraded. You can see the results in Figure 4.6.

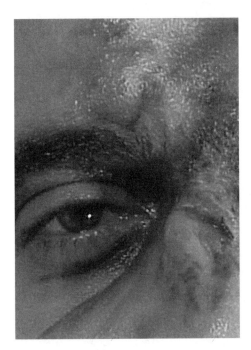

Figure 4.5   Combine mottling and blending to form a natural-looking bruise. (Model: Matt Harchick)

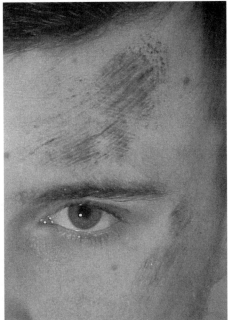

Figure 4.6   An abrasion is created with a simple swipe of a stipple sponge loaded with thick stage blood. (Model: John Imblis)

37

You can further enhance the effect by mottling with more blood to create the weepy look of a fresh, nasty scrape, as shown in Figure 4.7.

Sunburn

Sunburn can be re-created with a well-blended application of an appropriate shade of red to the area to be burned. However, for a higher degree of burn, you can reproduce blistering and peeling by applying a thin coat of latex to the skin first. Force it dry, then apply the makeup.

When the makeup is set, pinch and pull the latex to form blisters and areas of peeling, as shown in Figure 4.8.

To make the burn suppurate—that is, drippy—dab a little K-Y Jelly into the blistered areas.

Okay, so it's not all paint. So sue me.

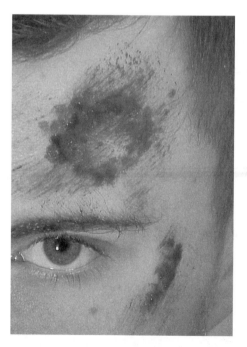

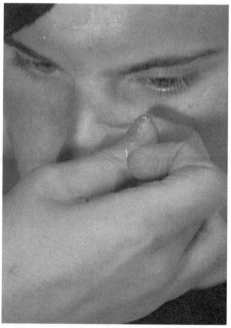

Figure 4.7   The same abrasion mottled with thick stage blood gives the appearance of a fresh, weeping wound. (Model: John Imblis)

Figure 4.8   A blistered, peeling sunburn is as simple as a coating of latex followed by a red foundation or crème color. (Model: John Imblis)

Third-Degree Burn

A third-degree burn is one in which the epidermal layers have been burned away by fire or heat. It leaves subcutaneous tissue, including the yellowing layer of fat, exposed.

Third-degree burns can be easily reproduced with paint techniques, as shown in Figure 4.9. This uses a combination of paint techniques, including mottling to get the outer rim of deep red and stippling to give the textured look to the inner yellow/ white and yellow/brown. The outer edge also uses some veining, as well as a combination of blending techniques to get the burn to fade gradually into the healthy skin around it.

To add a little extra texture to the burn in Figure 4.9, we applied it over a thin coating of latex that was slightly picked and peeled.

This burn has been treated medically, meaning the charred epidermis has been removed. For a fresher, crisper look, you could apply additional latex over the burn to peel and pull and create flaps of skin. You would then dress them with black makeup and dust them with charcoal powder to make them look really charred.

As with the sunburn, you can make the burn suppurate with K-Y Jelly, pectin, or gelatin (preparing and using pectin and gelatin is covered in the next chapter).

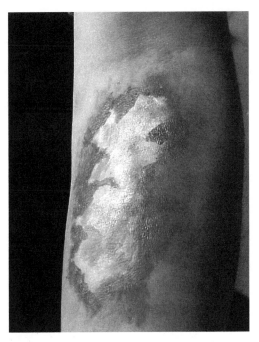

Figure 4.9   A third-degree burn done in paint, with a little latex for texture.

Combining Effects: Frozen

To demonstrate the range of possibilities available from a handful of simple techniques, we've taken the makeup from Chapter 9, "Ghostly Visage," and modified it slightly. Both are essentially painted effects with some 3-D dressing.

To accomplish this makeup, you'll execute the step-by-step instructions for the makeup in Chapter 9, omitting the fluorescent underpainting and contact lenses.

Instead, when the makeup itself is complete, you'll drizzle your model with Scar Effects Gel to simulate ice. You can also use your own gelatin concoction or a commercial product like Ultra Ice to complete the effect. Sprinkle liberally with fake snow; we used white wax shavings, but soap or plastic snow will work, too.

The effect is a rather frightening, frozen cadaver, as shown in Figure 4.10—a little tribute to the late, great Stanley Kubrick.

You'll find through your own experimentation—coming up with variations on makeup designs presented here and those of your own—that a few simple changes to a design can produce a significantly different effect. That's why makeup artists, like magicians, guard their secrets so closely.

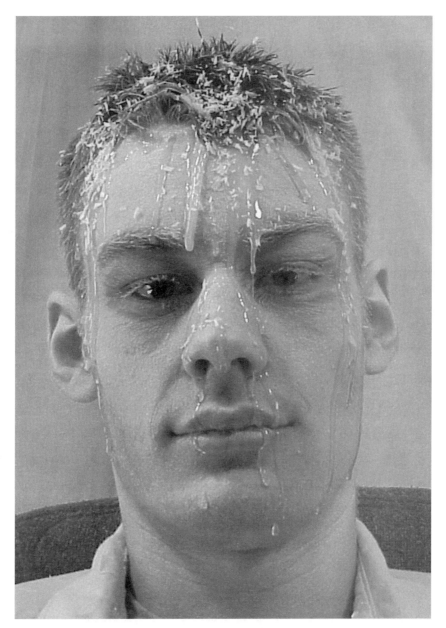

Figure 4.10   This frozen cadaver is a basic paint makeup, dressed with Scar Effects Gel and some wax scrapings. (Model: John McGurl)

5
3-D Effects

Paint is an excellent tool that can lend vitality and interesting detail to any makeup; however, some effects just don't work (or work as well) for an audience unless they're dimensional. A believable swollen bruise on an actor's forehead, done in paint, will reveal itself to be paint when the actor turns his or her head to the side and there's no actual lump.

There are a number of tools available to the makeup artist to create dimensional effects that will look realistic when viewed from any angle. This chapter will introduce you to the basic tools in your bag of tricks and show you how to work with them, and later chapters will demonstrate their flexibility with a number of different full-face makeup effects.

Mortician's Wax

Mortician's wax is more commonly known as nose putty or nose and scar wax. No matter what the manufacturer chooses to call it, however, it's still the same stuff that morticians use to rebuild damaged portions of a cadaver's face before an open-casket viewing.

Mortician's wax is a sticky, pliable substance that can easily be sculpted into just about any shape imaginable. It comes in several flesh tones, primarily Caucasian. It's perfect for its intended mortuary use because, frankly, corpses don't move very much. When used on the living, you may need to supplement the wax's inherent stickiness by applying it to a base coat of liquid latex and then finish the effect with a sealing coat of latex as well. Mortician's wax works best when applied to bonier areas that don't move much: the nose, the forehead, the temple, the cheekbones, the forearms, and the like.

Once applied, mortician's wax can be made up with the rest of the face, but care must be used to select an oil-based liquid foundation or rubber mask grease so the wax will be covered evenly.

Handling Mortician's Wax

Because of its inherent stickiness, mortician's wax will be difficult to work with unless you first coat your hands and sculpting tools with a thin coat of petroleum jelly, baby oil, or K-Y Jelly. Reapply as necessary, when the wax starts to stick to your fingers.

Once coated, working with the wax is much like working with Play-Doh or any other sculpting material. You can now rough out the general shape of the piece to be applied. Apply it to the base of liquid latex on the actor's face, then refine, shape, and sculpt the wax into its final form. Then thin and blend the edges of the wax into the actor's skin to minimize the appearance of seams before finishing the makeup.

You can use your fingers, the handle of a makeup brush, or just about anything to sculpt mortician's wax; however, we have found that a clay sculpting tool like the one shown in Figure 5.1 makes working with wax much easier. Most makeup supply houses sell them, but you can also find them in most art and craft supply stores.

To lend a more lifelike appearance to the finished wax appliance, you can apply skin texture to it by using texture stamps sold by most makeup supply houses. On the other hand, if you're cheap like us, you can simply roll the outside of a piece of citrus rind over the wax; the texture of an orange or lemon rind is very similar to that of human skin. You can also stipple the wax with a clean, dry, stiff-bristled brush.

Texture stamping is necessary for intimate theaters and for film and video work, where the difference in texture between skin and wax is easily noticed and can spoil your illusion.

As you experiment with mortician's wax, try various items you find and see how they work as texture stamps; just about any solid with surface detail will add texture to wax, and you never know when one of them will come in handy. As always, document your findings for future reference.

Figure 5.1   A clay sculpting tool can be your best friend while working with mortician's wax.

Typical Uses

In most day-to-day makeup designs, mortician's wax is commonly used to reshape noses and chins and to add the occasional cut or scar. The examples that follow will give you basic hands-on experience in creating these traditional wax effects.

For all of these basic effects, you'll need

⮑ Mortician's wax

⮑ Liquid latex

⮑ Hair dryer

⮑ Vaseline

⮑ Standard makeup supplies, including your bruise wheel and some stage blood

You'll learn very quickly that the application of the wax remains constant, no matter what you're doing with it. The difference between each of these effects is simply the shape into which you sculpt the wax and what makeup you dress it up with after the fact.

Once you're more familiar with the strengths and weaknesses of the wax, you'll think of new and interesting uses for this versatile tool.

Broken Nose   To build a broken nose, follow these simple steps:

1. Apply a coat of liquid latex to the bridge of the nose.

2. Force it dry.

3. Form a small ball of mortician's wax and press it onto the latex, offset slightly to the side of the nose.

4. Blend the edges of the wax into the actor's skin by thinning and shaving the edges with the flat end of the sculpting tool.

5. Blot any remnants of Vaseline from the surface of the mortician's wax.

6. Make up the wax and surrounding tissues of the nose with a bruise, using the paint techniques discussed in Chapter 4. Our finished product is shown in Figure 5.2.

Reshaping a Nose   To reshape an actor's nose, you'll follow a similar procedure; however, it isn't necessary to begin with a coat of latex, since the tip of the nose doesn't move that much.

1. Form a small ball of mortician's wax and press it onto the tip of the actor's nose.

2. Rough out the new nose shape, adding additional wax as necessary. Don't forget to reshape the nostrils.

3. Blend the edges of the wax into the actor's skin by thinning and shaving the edges with the flat end of the sculpting tool.

4. Blot any remnants of Vaseline from the surface of the mortician's wax.

5. Seal the wax with latex and force dry.

6. Make up the actor's nose to match the rest of the character's makeup. The nose we created is shown in Figure 5.3.

Reshaping a Chin The process of reshaping an actor's chin follows the same basic procedure. As with the nose, it isn't mandatory to start with a coating of liquid latex, since there isn't much give to most chins.

1. Form a medium-size ball of mortician's wax and press it into place on the actor's chin.

2. Sculpt the wax into the desired shape, adding additional wax as needed.

3. Blend the edges of the wax into the actor's skin by thinning and shaving the edges with the flat end of the sculpting tool.

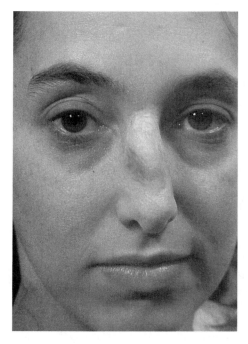

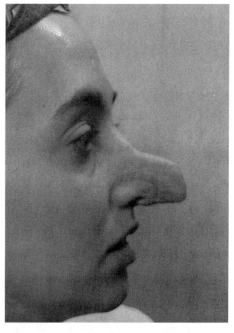

Figure 5.2   A broken nose built out of mortician's wax, as worn by our model Linda Eisen.

Figure 5.3   A brand-new nose, as modeled by Linda Eisen.

45

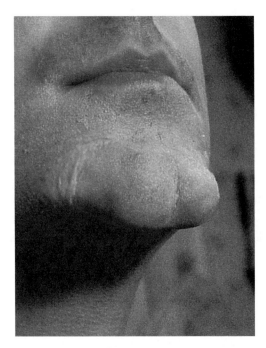

Figure 5.4   A cleft chin, as worn by makeup
artist and coauthor Dave Sartor.

4. Remove any traces of petroleum jelly from the mortician's wax.

5. Make up the actor's chin to fit the rest of the makeup. You can see our new chin in Figure 5.4.

Hematoma   *Hematoma* is doctor speak for a pool of blood that has built up in an area under the skin, outside of the circulatory system. Mortician's wax makes for a dandy hematoma.

1. Form a medium-size ball of mortician's wax and press it into place on the actor's head or forehead.

2. Sculpt the wax into the desired lump shape, adding additional wax as needed.

3. Blend the edges of the wax into the actor's skin by thinning and shaving the edges with the flat end of the sculpting tool.

4. Remove any leftover Vaseline from the wax.

5. Take a few moments to try texture stamping with citrus rinds, if you'd like. Just a suggestion.

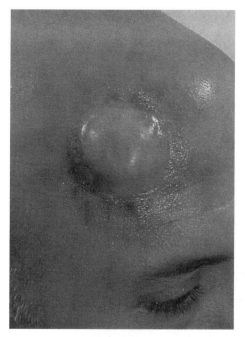 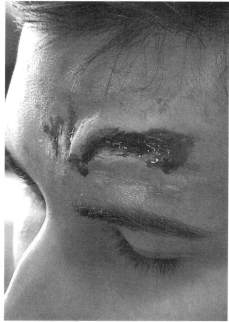

Figure 5.5   Quite a bump on the head, as worn by coauthor John Pivovarnick.

Figure 5.6   A nasty head wound, as worn by makeup artist and coauthor Dave Sartor.

6. Make up the hematoma to look freshly formed—a little bruised around the edges, with a nice highlight on the crown. Ours is shown in Figure 5.5.

Cuts and Scars   You can also use mortician's wax to create cuts and scars; however, there are simpler, more efficient ways to do these, as you'll see in the next section. The process for creating scars and cuts with wax is exactly the same as those described previously; but we're tired of typing them, so you *must* be sick of reading them. So, for a change, you'll see a finished gash in Figure 5.6, and we'll leave it to you to deconstruct it based on the previous examples.

Being able to deconstruct an effect you've seen is an excellent skill to develop. It reinforces your existing knowledge, gives you a good mental exercise, and makes it easy to expand upon the work of other makeup artists you've seen.

Rigid Collodion

Rigid collodion is *the* simplest and easiest way to build a very realistic scar or cut, in almost no time at all. It's a smelly chemical concoction that comes in the same sort of small, brush-in-the-lid bottles as nail polish.

To use it, you brush it on the actor's skin wherever you want to add a scar or a cut. It may take several coats, and you should allow each coat to dry before you apply the next. As the collodion dries, it contracts, pulling in the actor's skin and forming a very natural-looking hollow that can be dressed with makeup for a scar, or blood and makeup for a nasty-looking cut.

You can see samples of collodion at work in Figures 5.7 and 5.8. These effects were done with Michael Davy's Collodacolor line of colored collodion, which can, in many cases, save you from having to add any additional makeup to your effect.

Be aware that collodion is smelly, smelly stuff. It should be used in a well-ventilated area. Actors wearing collodion for an effect need to know how to remove it and how to care for their skin after the fact. That information is given in Appendix A, "Cleaning Up Your Act."

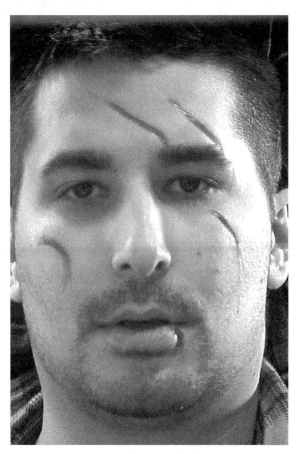

Figure 5.7   A few collodion scars without additional makeup, worn by Dave Sartor.

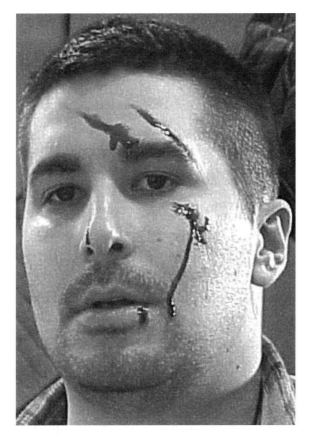

Figure 5.8   The same collodion scars dressed with
Fresh Scab and stage blood for a recent slash wound.

Shopper's alert: There are two varieties of collodion available: flexible and
rigid. You want *rigid* collodion, or your effect won't work.

Build Your Own Latex Appliances

In some cases, mortician's wax isn't appropriate for use, for example, when you have
a quick change, the effect must be placed on soft tissue, or you need a more durable
effect. Latex appliances often fill the bill.

While many latex appliances are available premade from makeup supply houses
(we used several from Burman Industries throughout the rest of this book), you might
not find exactly the one you need, or you might not want to spend the money on
them; they average about ten to twenty dollars a pop.

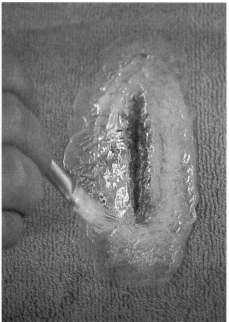

Figure 5.10   Once the base coat has dried, build up the details of the appliance—in this case, a slash wound—with latex and tissue.

Figure 5.11   You might want to precolor the appliance and let it dry well overnight.

The application of these homemade appliances is demonstrated in Chapter 12, if you're in a hurry to try yours out.

Teeth and Fangs

Some characters and creatures have, hmm, interesting dental needs. While there is nothing wrong with simply staining and/or blacking out an actor's teeth to help him portray a role, there is something to be said for completely changing the appearance of his teeth, particularly for character and creature makeups for which human teeth just won't *do*.

You can make dental appliances pretty easily. The teeth are inexpensive (especially compared to commercial products), easy to make, and a lot of fun.

In cases where the character in question has a speaking role, the teeth shown here may not be what you want; they are fitted appliances that will interfere to some degree with the actor's ability to speak. For principal roles, you may want to consider professionally constructed dental appliances that will have less of an impact on an actor's speech and diction. You can also construct partial plates that will interfere less with the actor's performance than the fitted appliances discussed here.

The teeth we're going to discuss were made from American Art Clay Company's Friendly Plastic, which is a nontoxic hard plastic with a low melting temperature. It comes in both stick and pellet versions and in a variety of colors. For the teeth, we used the white pellets. You can find Friendly Plastic at large art supply stores and in supply catalogs such as that of Burman Industries.

Materials

To make these false teeth, you'll need the following supplies:

- Friendly Plastic, white
- Realistic teeth—you can either buy some from dental and/or taxidermy supply houses, depending on the sort of teeth you want, or you can sculpt any sort of teeth you want from Friendly Plastic
- Nontoxic permanent markers in assorted colors, including red, yellow, brown, and green
- Hot-melt glue gun and glue sticks
- Dremel or similar rotary tool
- Precision knife
- Small saucepan of boiling water
- Cold water
- Slotted spoon

Preparation

Before you begin constructing your teeth, bring a pan of water to boil. Drop in about half a cup of Friendly Plastic. The white pellets will turn clear, which tells you the plastic is ready to work with.

Carefully remove the plastic from the water using the slotted spoon. Let it cool for a second or two, blot it dry, then color it with the red marker. Work the color through the plastic by kneading. You're tinting the plastic you'll use for the gums of your dentures; you'll also get an idea of how long you have to work with the plastic before it cools down and hardens again. Don't worry though, you can drop the plastic right back into hot water and it will soften right up—that's one of the nice things about Friendly Plastic.

Construction

When you're ready to begin, reheat the colored Friendly Plastic.

1. Let the plastic cool enough to handle. Take about half the amount, and form it into a snake about one-half inch in diameter.

2. Carefully press it over your upper teeth and wrap it around to the back. Work it up to the ridge of the gum line. Don't go too high, though, or you'll have a heck of time getting it out again.

> If you *do* have trouble getting the plastic free of your teeth, you can soften up the plastic by swirling warm water around in your mouth and then try again. Sometimes it takes a few tries to get it right.

3. While it's in place, swirl cold water around in your mouth to hurry the cooling process.

4. Carefully remove the plastic from your teeth. Rinse in cold water and set aside. You can see a sample plate in Figure 5.12.

5. Repeat steps 1 through 4 for the lower teeth.

6. Once you have the gums made, clean up any rough or sharp edges by trimming with a precision knife. You can also bur them off with the rotary tool. You can smooth the trimmed area by dipping the plastic briefly in hot water until the outer layer softens and relaxes; this will also remove any fingerprints.

7. Refit the gums in your mouth and mark the center line and the level where your lips are when you smile. These marks will guide your placement of the teeth.

8. Remove the gums and let dry.

9. Using the hot-melt glue gun, begin gluing the teeth into position on the upper plate, as shown in Figure 5.13. You need only about six teeth on each plate, especially if you're adding large fangs.

10. When the upper plate is done, match it up with the lower plate to see where the lower teeth should go; mark the lower gum as a reminder. You don't want upper and lower teeth colliding, as they will pop off.

11. Glue the teeth to the lower plate, following the guidelines you've drawn. Retest the positioning of the teeth, as shown in Figure 5.14.

12. Try them on for size and comfort. Adjust as necessary.

13. If desired, color and stain the teeth with nontoxic permanent markers. You can see several finished pairs of homemade teeth in Figure 5.15.

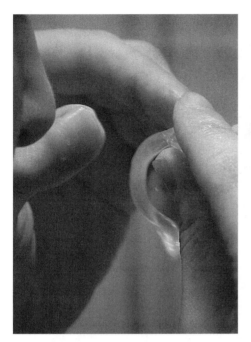

Figure 5.12   Making the gums for your teeth is much like fitting an athletic mouth guard. Be sure to trim any rough edges before proceeding.

Figure 5.13   Use a hot-melt glue gun to glue the teeth into place on the upper plate, starting at the center and working out on each side.

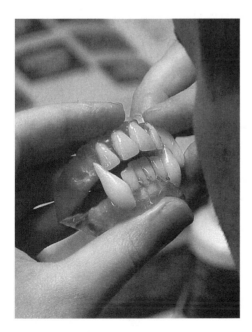

Figure 5.14   Positioning the teeth correctly is essential. Check frequently, and reposition the teeth as necessary.

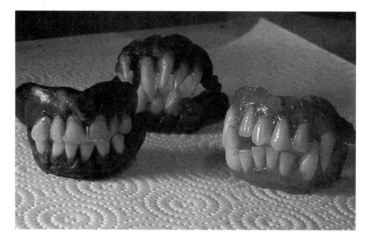

Figure 5.15   An assortment of dental appliances using both storebought and sculpted teeth.

You can sculpt any sort of teeth, including fangs, from Friendly Plastic; simply sculpt the soft plastic with your fingers into whatever shape you want, then drop them into a glass of cold water to set.

Teeth, while not an absolute necessity for an effects makeup, are an excellent finishing touch that can make the rest of the makeup really pop.

Unexplored Dimensions

Three-dimensional makeup is uncharted territory for many makeup artists, simply because the need hasn't arisen for it. There are, however, many opportunities, in the most mundane of productions, to experiment and explore the advantages and disadvantages of incorporating simple dimensional effects into your designs.

The best preparation for executing a dimensional makeup that is essential to a production is to play with three-dimensional effects well in advance of the need. You'll get a feel for what they can bring to your designs, and it will get you to start thinking dimensionally while in the design phase, even if you don't end up incorporating a dimensional effect into your design.

Then, when the need for a dimensional effect comes up, you'll be prepared to cope with it.

6
Blood and Other Effects

$\mathcal{I}$n the world of effects makeup, artists are frequently called upon to come up with new and interesting secretions with which to slather actors—blood, pus, scabs, and other oozy, crusty creations.

This chapter gives you a general primer for blood and related effects, including a commercial product overview as well as recipes for making your own. You'll also get some delivery techniques that are useful for when you need blood and other fluids to appear onstage, or in front of the camera, on cue.

Blood and Blood By-Products

Blood is by far the most commonly used bodily fluid onstage. Makeup companies produce it in a variety of formulations for a variety of uses.

Whenever you're working with any quantity of blood onstage, you should work with the costume designer to be sure that there will be either an ample supply of replacement costume pieces or regular laundry sessions to clean garments that have been stained by blood. Artificial blood stains, depending on the type and brand, can be almost as difficult to get out of clothes as the real thing.

Some stage blood products—particularly the cheap, squeeze-tube variety that gets sold around Halloween—can stain both clothes and skin. Always test your blood products on both skin and fabric to see how much staining will happen, *before* you commit to using it for a run.

Blood Types

Well, there's O, O positive . . .

Actually, there are a variety of commercial blood products available. What follows is a list of the different types and their more common uses.

➲ Stage blood—a liquid, free-flowing version typically used for any effect where blood needs to flow freely or drip. It comes in edible and nonedible formulations. The edible formulas, of course, are designed for use in an actor's mouth—blood capsules and the like—for the sudden appearance of blood after a gunshot or other attack. It can be harmlessly swallowed and comes in a variety of flavors

> Because stage blood is water-based, it will bead up on latex appliances and greasepaint. When applying stage blood to such surfaces, you can minimize beading by adding a few drops of liquid dish soap to the blood. The dish soap breaks the surface tension of the blood, reducing the amount of beading.

➲ Gel blood—a less free-flowing version of stage blood used to dress fresh wounds, but with less running and dripping. It's used where you need more control of the positioning of the blood, particularly in film and video, where free-flowing blood poses a continuity problem

➲ Thick blood—an even thicker, stay-put formulation that's best for dressing wounds where you don't want the blood to move at all. It comes in several formulations, including thick blood, fresh scab, and scab

➲ A/B blood—a special-effects treat. A/B blood is a two-part solution of chemicals (part a and part b, hence the name) that are, by themselves, colorless. However, when you mix them together, you get a brilliant red blood color. Typically, you'd apply one part to the actor, wherever the blood is supposed to appear, and the other part to a knife, or whatever will be producing the injury. When you drag the treated knife over the treated skin, the chemicals combine and create a very realistic cut effect. The chemicals have a waterlike consistency, which makes delivery very easy—you can even load it in squirt guns. The possible uses for A/B blood are limited only by your imagination

Custom Colors

Most stage blood comes in basic blood red. However, blood takes on different properties and colors depending on where it is in the circulatory system when it's released. Heart blood, for example, is a very dark red. Blood from the lungs is a brilliant red, since it's just been oxygenated.

You can recolor commercial stage blood by adding liquid food coloring to get the exact shade of blood you need for a particular effect. It's best to experiment with coloring a small quantity of blood, keeping track of the proportions you've used (document everything) so that you can easily reproduce any colors, in any size batch, whenever you need to.

Depending on the lighting gels that are being used for a particular production, you might want to experiment with several shades of blood onstage to see which coloration gives you the best visual effect.

You can also change the consistency of the stage blood by adding talcum powder or cornstarch. It both thickens the blood and renders it opaque.

Blood Substitutes

Depending on your need, and your use of the blood, you may want to substitute another substance for the typical blood products available. For example, in black-and-white photography (both still and motion), chocolate syrup looks more bloodlike than any prepared products—and it's definitely edible.

Just about any syrup in an appropriate shade of red will make a passable blood substitute. Black currant syrup—usually available in Chinese food stores—is excellent. Wilton cake dyes can also be used, either as a blood substitute or as a blood coloring. Chocolate syrup tinted with a tiny bit of red also makes an excellent dried blood.

With food products, as well as prepared blood, you should experiment to see what's going to work best for you and to see which products will stain either the actor's clothes or his skin before use in an actual production. While food substitutes for blood have the bonus of tasting better than edible blood, they also tend to stain more.

Make Your Own Blood

Effects makeup artists tend to guard their various blood recipes the same way chefs guard the recipe for the specialty a la maison. The recipes that follow are for basic blood and some related bodily fluids and secretions that you can use as a starting place to develop your own secret mix.

The basic blood recipe, like many effects recipes, is done more by look and feel than by actual measurements. As you experiment, document your steps so you can reproduce your recipe whenever you need it.

Basic Blood

➲ Karo corn syrup—light or dark, depending on how dark you want your final blood to be

➲ Red food coloring—a lot of it

➲ 1–2 drops of yellow food coloring

➲ 1–2 drops of green food coloring

Pour the corn syrup into a bowl or bottle, then add the red food coloring until it reaches a suitably bloody shade. Add a drop or two each of the yellow and green food coloring to deepen the color. Adjust the color by adding small amounts of additional food coloring until you hit the shade you need.

This recipe gives you a serviceable, completely edible—and tasty—blood. Depending on your needs, however, you may want a thicker or more opaque blood; then you might want to add unscented talcum powder or cornstarch. If you want the blood to remain edible, stick with cornstarch.

If the blood is for use on greasepaint or latex appliances, you will also want to add two drops of liquid dish soap. Keep in mind, however, that the addition of soap renders the blood inedible.

When creating your own stage blood—or any make-your-own makeup product—it is absolutely essential that you store it in a sealed jar and label the contents. You don't want to wonder if a bottle of blood is edible or not. You should also date each jar, so you know how long it's been sitting on your shelf.

Lung/Arterial Blood

To create lung blood—the sort coughed up after a gunshot to the chest or other chest trauma—follow the same recipe as for basic blood, omitting the green and yellow food coloring. Lung blood tends to be a much brighter red than your run-of-the-mill blood, as does blood from an artery, because it's been recently oxygenated.

Heart/Vascular Blood

To create heart blood—the darker blood you'd see after a gunshot wound to the heart or during open heart surgery—follow the same recipe as for basic blood, *adding extra green and yellow food coloring*.

The darker blood is also good for vascular blood, because the vascular system returns oxygen-depleted blood to the lungs to be reoxygenated, so it has a darker appearance.

Thick Blood, Slime, and Other Ooze

There are two ways to get an effective thick blood, slime, or other ooziness: by using a thick, unflavored gelatin or by using pectin.

Gelatin   Knox unflavored gelatin can be cooked into a supersaturated solution using roughly six packets of Knox to a cup or so of water. Simmer until it reaches a puddinglike consistency.

It can then be colored with food coloring, water-based paint, or makeup. There are some suggested color combinations in the pectin section that you can try with gelatin as well.

To keep the gelatin workable, it can be reheated on the stove or in a microwave or kept over a low heat in a double boiler.

To increase the durability of a gelatin concoction, you can substitute glycerin for half of the quantity of water.

Pectin   Pectin is used as a natural thickening agent in many food products, particularly jellies and jams. It can be acquired in any supermarket that carries canning supplies and is sold under various brand names (Sure-Jell and Smucker's Pectin, for example).

A basic recipe for a small batch of pectin-based slime:

- ⮑ 1 packet of powdered pectin
- ⮑ ½ cup water
- ⮑ 2 or more tablespoons of sugar
- ⮑ Assorted food coloring

In a small saucepan, combine the water and pectin and bring it to a boil. Add one to two tablespoons of sugar; the more sugar you add, the thicker your final product. Boil for one minute.

Remove the pan from the heat and add whatever coloration you want to:

⊃ Red with a touch of brown for a fresh scab

⊃ Red with a touch of yellow and green for thick blood

⊃ White with a touch of yellow for pus

⊃ Green for pond scum slime

⊃ Nothing for a clear, *Alien*-ish mouth slime

You can also texturize your slime creations with solids to suit your needs: add raw or cooked rice for maggoty slime; oatmeal for vomit; cream cheese and black cherry jam for a very nasty (and tasty) afterbirth. Use your imagination, and play.

If you don't care to go through all the hassle of experimenting with your own slimy creations, there are commercial products (UltraSlime, UltraIce, and others) that you can buy and tinker with.

You can also start with a base of methylcellulose, a common food additive available from commercial bakery supply houses and theatrical and film effects supply houses (like Burman Industries).

Delivery Techniques

Special-effects makeup, being the crazy quilt of disciplines that it is, often treads on the toes of other creative departments. Technically, some of the delivery methods available fall firmly in the lap of the prop person, but it's still good for the makeup artist to know them, particularly when working with smaller companies where there may not be an official prop person.

Other delivery methods, such as blood bags loaded with small explosive squibs, fall into the realm of pyrotechnics and require special training. Because of the dangerous nature of any explosive charge onstage, no matter how small, that will *not* be covered here.

Capsules

For flowing effects, where small amounts of blood—or other substances—must flow from an actor's mouth, the tried-and-true delivery method is by gelatin capsule.

You can purchase empty capsules from most makeup supply houses, which you then fill with the ooze of your choice. The actor pockets or palms the capsule(s), then, just before the big moment, surreptitiously pops one or two in her mouth. When the liquid must flow, she bites the capsule, releasing the effect.

Blood Bags

When larger quantities of blood are needed, you can create blood bags. You can work with any basic sandwich bag that is thin enough, or plain cellophane wrap.

> To test a bag to see if it's thin enough, fill one with water and seal it. Hold it over the sink and squeeze. If it pops, it's thin enough.

Fill the bag with an ample amount of blood. Use very thin blood, especially if it must bleed through a costume. Thin some stage blood with a little water. Twist the bag until the blood is squeezed into one corner and the bag is almost ready to pop. Seal the bag with tape—electrical tape works well—and trim off any excess bag. Affix the bag to the actor or his costume, somewhere out of sight. When the moment comes, a gunshot for example, the actor clutches the appropriate area and squeezes the blood bag until it bursts, delivering the blood. The actor may also palm the blood bag and squeeze when needed.

When using with blood bags, you should give the actor a few to play with before rehearsal so he or she can get used to working with them.

Blade Techniques

You can rig just about any large-handled, bladed weapon—knife or old-fashioned straight razor—to deliver blood by using a small bulb, like the kind they sell as ear syringes in the baby departments of most drugstores.

First, remove the cutting edge from any bladed weapon. You can grind it off with a rotary tool or a power drill with a grinding stone tip or take it to a professional knife sharpener and have it dulled there. Safety first.

Fill a bulb syringe with thick blood, which is easier to control. Attach the bulb to the handle of the knife or razor so that it is hidden or can be hidden by the hand of the actor using it. The tip of the bulb should be fixed at the spot on the blade where it will begin cutting.

As the actor cuts someone, he or she squeezes the bulb and releases blood on the victim's throat (or wherever), and draws the knife through it, leaving a blade-thin trail of blood that looks like cut skin to the audience.

The actor will need rehearsal time with the knife to coordinate the cutting with the squeezing to get a fast, effortless effect.

A Basic Garrote

You can build a basic garrote like the ones used in *Deathtrap* and other thrillers from two pieces of dowel (about five inches each) and some black yarn or cotton cord (about a foot). Attach the yarn to one end of each dowel (you can sculpt the dowel into any shape you like) using a carpet tack or a thumbtack.

Dip the black yarn in blood and wring out any excess. You don't want it dripping, simply damp.

When an actor mimes strangling someone with the garrote, the blood (hidden in the black yarn) is released on the victim's neck, making for a very effective strangling.

The actor will definitely need coaching on using the garrote effectively. You don't want any real pressure inflicted on the victim's throat, nor do you want any misses with the placement of the garrote—blood appearing anywhere else (on a forehead, say) will kill the effect, not the victim.

Syringe Techniques

Flowing blood is always effective onstage. One way to get blood flowing freely is to use a needleless syringe and a small-gauge air hose, available anywhere that sells aquarium supplies. Syringes can be purchased in a variety of sizes from effects supply houses, or you can go to the wallpaper section of your favorite paint or hardware store and buy a syringe used to remove air bubbles from behind wallpaper.

The basic theory is that you run the air hose to wherever you want the blood delivered on the actor's body, then use the syringe to deliver it. In theory, it's dandy. However, the rigging of it is another matter. It takes time and experimentation to rig the effect so it works. Some key concepts you need to keep in mind include the following:

➲ You need a sufficient volume of blood, so that enough arrives at the destination to achieve the desired effect, which means using a large enough syringe, filling the air tube with blood in advance, or using another method of propelling the blood that allows for a larger blood reservoir.

➲ Allow enough travel time for the blood (or whatever liquid) to get to its destination on cue and/or load the tubing with enough blood so that the slightest pressure on the syringe's plunger sends it gushing out.

➲ If you're filling the air hose with blood to facilitate delivery, then you need to seal the end of the tube with putty or another substance that will give you a good seal but pop out when the plunger is pressed.

➲ Typically, the effect must be self-contained, so that the actor can move freely about the stage and operate the effect unnoticeably (or have it rigged so that a nearby actor can press in the plunger). Or, the scene must be staged to get the actor to a spot where he or she can pick up the air hose a moment or two before it is engaged by a stagehand offstage.

The theory is all well and good; however, nothing replaces hands-on experimentation. In the section that follows, you'll see a simple stigmata effect that uses the syringe technique, from which you may extrapolate an effect as elaborate as you care to create.

Stigmata 101

Stigmata, if you missed the movie, is a physical manifestation of the wounds Christ suffered on the cross in a person of unwavering faith. It appears in many Christian pageants and in some mainstream theater pieces like *Agnes of God*.

While there are many possible ways to create a stigmata effect, this one demonstrates the syringe technique discussed earlier.

Materials

To execute this one-armed stigmata, you will need the following supplies:

- ⊃ Blood
- ⊃ Air tubing, about a yard
- ⊃ Wallpaper syringe, without needle
- ⊃ 1½″- or 2″-wide surgical tape
- ⊃ Liquid foundation or rubber mask grease to match the actor's skin tone
- ⊃ Bruise wheel
- ⊃ Highlight wheel
- ⊃ Flesh Effects Gel (or your own gelatin concoction, as discussed earlier in this chapter)

Preparation

To begin, you'll need to measure the actor on whom the effect will be created. You need to have enough air hose to run from the actor's wrist, along the inside of his arm, over the shoulder, to wherever the syringe of blood will be hidden.

> For a production, you would work with the costume designer to make sure that sleeves will hide most, if not all, of the actor's arms. There might even be the possibility of building the air hose into the costume.

You might also want to experiment with bloods of different thicknesses to see which best suits your needs; thinner blood flows better than thick blood, but it also runs off very quickly once delivered.

To get a leak-free joint between the syringe and the tubing, dip the end of the tubing into hot water, then, while the tubing is still soft, fit it to the end of the syringe where the needle screws on. You'll be able to remove and replace the tubing, but you'll have a pretty tight seal. If the seal loosens, simply repeat the process again.

You can also use hot water to straighten the tubing, if you buy it bundled into a small package; just pull the tubing through a pan of hot water, and it will straighten right out.

While you've got the hot water, you need to heat up the effects gel so it is free-flowing. Put the bottle in a pan of recently boiled water to loosen it up.

Just before you're ready to begin, you can apply surgical tape to the air hose. You want the air hose running down the center of the tape, and you want the tape as smooth as possible, at least at the wrist end of the tube, where a wrinkle will tip the audience off.

The Effect

To begin, you'll tape the air hose to the actor's arm.

1. Run the air hose from the actor's wrist, up the inner arm a few inches, then around the outer arm up to the shoulder, and over.

2. Test to make sure the actor can freely bend his arm without kinking the air hose; if he cannot, reapply the air hose, leaving a little excess at the elbow.

3. Secure the air hose with the surgical tape. For a secure fit, you can add additional tape wherever the tube will be hidden by costume. You can see an applied air hose in Figure 6.1.

4. Apply foundation to the surgical tape and blend it into the actor's skin.

5. Next, around the wrist end of the air hose, begin building a pool for the blood to collect in, using the Flesh Effects Gel—it's just like making that dent in your mashed potatoes to hold the gravy.

6. Since stigmata tends to reoccur, heal, and scar, you may want to dress the Flesh Effects Gel to resemble old scars, as in the blood pool shown in Figure 6.2.

7. Load the syringe with blood.

8. Attach the syringe to the back end of the air hose.

9. Fire when ready, preferably over a bucket or sink. You can see ours spurt in Figure 6.3; however, it isn't as effective in a still image as it is live and in person.

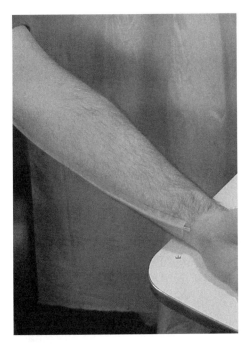

Figure 6.1   Attach the air hose to the actor's arm from wrist to shoulder, making sure there's enough slack for him to bend his elbow freely.

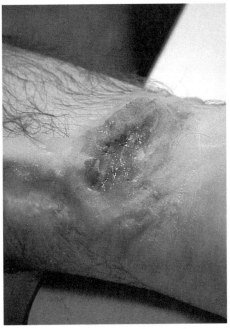

Figure 6.2   Build a pool in which the blood will collect using Flesh Effects Gel. Dress it with makeup to resemble an old scar.

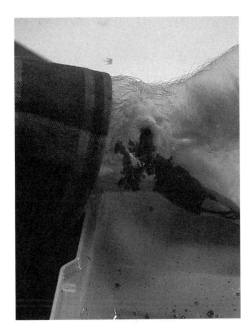

Figure 6.3   Pushing the plunger on the syringe delivers the blood to the wrist wound, where it wells up before spilling to the floor.

It will take some playing to see how slowly, or quickly, the actor will need to depress the plunger to send the blood flying. He will want to go slowly enough that the blood collects in the pool you build with effects gel, which also doubles as the nail hole.

Naturally, to fully duplicate the stigmata effect, you'd have to repeat the process on the actor's other arm. Then you would probably want to use a three-way gang valve (also available at pet stores) so that both wrist wounds would feed off the same syringe.

After you're through with the effect, run warm water through the air hose to clean out any residual stage blood. You don't want it drying in there and restricting blood flow later.

Bloody Thoughts

When it comes to working with blood onstage, particularly in the area of delivery, there isn't much in the way of right and wrong—only what works and what doesn't. While there are some tried-and-true methods of delivering blood on cue, most techniques were made up as different productions posed different problems and refined when those techniques didn't work for other productions, which is probably why effects artists carefully guard many of their blood secrets. They worked hard to discover them.

Part 3
Full-Face Effects

Now that you have an understanding of the core FX techniques under your belt, it's time to play mix-and-match.

The full-face effects that follow all elaborate on the basic skills covered previously. You'll find yourself combining them to create such disparate effects as a realistic, dimensional age makeup and a horrible disfiguration by fire or acid, both using variations on the same techniques.

7
Dimensional Old Age

T raditionally, the preferred method for aging an actor for a role has been the standard set of paint techniques that have been available since makeup was invented.

Depending on the age of the actor and the target age you're trying to reach, simple paint techniques may not be enough, particularly in school circumstances, where your pool of actors generally doesn't contain anyone over the age of twenty-two.

Many plays popular in educational settings require older actors that simply may not be available: *The American Dream*, *The Effect of Gamma Rays on Man-in-the-Moon Marigolds*, *Driving Miss Daisy*, and *Arsenic and Old Lace*, to name a few.

Coupled with a talented actor, the makeup that follows can provide you with an effective and believable older character.

Materials

To execute this makeup, you will need

- ➲ White and silver temporary hair color, or an appropriate wig
- ➲ Prosthetic eye bags, available from most makeup and costume supply houses
- ➲ Liquid latex
- ➲ Pros-Aide
- ➲ Adhesive Blending Paste
- ➲ Greasepaint or rubber mask grease in a suitable foundation shade
- ➲ Age stipple wheel
- ➲ Shadow wheel

71

➲ Lip color

➲ Neutral eye shadow

➲ Pressed powder blush

➲ Makeup sponges

➲ Brushes

➲ Cotton swabs

➲ Toothbrush

➲ Hair dryer

➲ Small pair of scissors

➲ Bond Off! or Detach-All for removal

The foam latex eye bags should be of a size appropriate to the actor's face. They are typically sold in small, medium, and large sizes.

Preparation

It's helpful if you spray the actor's hair with the temporary hair color *before* you begin the actual face makeup—that way, if there's any overspray on the face, it will wipe right off with a damp towel, without destroying your makeup.

We call for two colors of spray, white and silver. We've found it useful, particularly when covering dark hair, to use the white spray as sort of a primer coat, followed by an application of the silver. It gets you better coverage overall, and you get a more natural-looking blend of colors, rather than a solid helmet of either silver or white.

Once the spray is on and dry, get the actor's hair up and out of the way of the face; there's nothing more annoying than to have a few loose hairs glued to your face during a performance.

Naturally, if you're opting for a wig, you can simply put up the actor's hair and get on with the makeup.

Before you begin, you should also take a look at the foam latex appliances. Sometimes they come with excess latex around the edges caused by leakage when the molds were injected. You *do* want a thin edge of latex around the appliance because it helps blend the latex into the skin (that's why it's called the blending edge), but you should carefully trim away any obviously extraneous latex from the edges.

The Makeup

To begin, we're going to attach the foam latex appliances.

1. Apply a thin coat of Pros-Aide to the area under the actor's eyes and the back of the latex eye bags. Give the Pros-Aide a moment or two to set up.

2. Carefully position the latex eye bags and press into place.

3. Use some Adhesive Blending Paste to smooth the seam between the eye bag and the actor's skin; it works just like spackle. It blends easily with a moist sponge or wet cotton swab. You can see the positioning of the eye bags and the application of the blending paste in Figure 7.1.

4. Apply a coat of liquid latex to the actor's forehead.

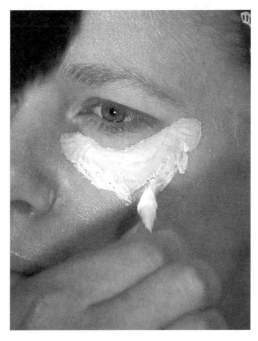

Figure 7.1   Carefully apply the under-eye appliances with Pros-Aide or another adhesive. Mask the seams using a little Adhesive Blending Paste.

5. While stretching the actor's skin up toward the top of the head, force the latex dry with a hair dryer. The stretching is important, as the dried latex will then contract, forming your wrinkles.

Whenever you're using latex to form wrinkles this way, stretch in the opposite direction of how you want your wrinkles to form: if you want horizontal wrinkles, stretch the skin vertically; for vertical wrinkles, stretch horizontally. Also keep in mind that the resulting wrinkles depend on the amount of stretch in the actor's skin. Just a little stretch will give you shallow wrinkles. More stretch gives deeper wrinkles.

6. Repeat steps 4 and 5 on the planes of each cheek, pulling the skin tight toward the ears as you force the latex dry.

7. Do the same again at the corner of each eye, stretching the skin both up and down as you force the latex dry. This will create a nice web of crow's feet.

8. If necessary to achieve your desired level of wrinkles, you may apply additional coats of latex on each of the areas and force them dry again. Figure 7.2 shows the amount of wrinkling achieved in two coats of latex.

You can dramatically increase the amount of wrinkling you get from this effect by adding a layer of bathroom tissue to the latex. Latex the skin, lay on pieces of tissue, and then coat the tissue with more latex. Stretch the skin and tissue while forcing the latex dry. The addition of the tissue will wrinkle even the tightest, youngest skin.

9. When the latex is completely dry, apply a foundation of greasepaint or rubber mask grease over all. For our makeup, we used two colors of greasepaint, a light shade and a medium shade, blended by a brush on the model's face—an easy way to achieve the mottled look of some older skin.

10. Carefully draw the foundation color up to the eyes and lids using a brush or a sponge.

11. Highlight the brow bone and eyelids.

12. Draw shadow color into prominent wrinkles to accent—forehead, beside mouth, and around eyes.

Figure 7.2   After stretching and force drying
the latex, it should pull the actor's skin into a
nice pattern of wrinkles.

13. Shade the hollows of the cheeks, using brush strokes rather than a blended shadow—it lends a wrinkled texture to the makeup. You can see what I mean in Figure 7.3.

14. Sponge foundation color over shadow areas to clean up the lines of shadow and leave color only in the wrinkle creases.

15. Retouch shadows as necessary.

16. Highlight prominent shadow areas. The application of highlight and shadow, including those isolated to the wrinkle folds with the application of foundation, can be seen in Figure 7.4.

17. Powder to set.

18. Add lip color. With a fine brush, you can insinuate the lipstick bleed effect some older women get when lipstick is drawn into the fine wrinkles around their mouths.

19. Make up eyes in neutral browns and beiges.

20. Gray the eyebrows with colored hairspray by spraying the color onto an old toothbrush and brushing it into the brows.

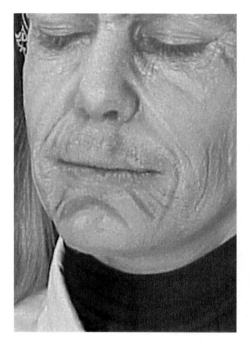

Figure 7.3   The highlight and shadow should be applied to bring out the wrinkles formed by the dried latex.

Figure 7.4   Even though the makeup is dimensional, the careful application of highlight and shadow is necessary to bring out the full effect of the latex wrinkles.

The toothbrush method is also an excellent way to apply subtle color to someone's hair. You can get streaks of gray or even a general salt-and-pepper effect. It's also handy for touching up the roots of sprayed hair, as well as for coloring beards and mustaches without the risks of overspray.

21. Lightly apply blush to cheeks, chin, and brow bone.

22. Touch up hair color and style hair (or add your wig).

You can see the final makeup in Figure 7.5. As with any effects makeup, lighting is critical; compare the difference in the chin area in Figures 7.4 and 7.5, brought on by a simple readjustment of the lighting.

For this makeup, we went for a well-tended matron in street makeup. If we were doing this for a woman who wouldn't wear much in the way of makeup, we would have added an assortment of age/liver spots and possibly some fine red veins near the nose and possibly a blue one on the forehead.

Figure 7.5   The final dimensional age makeup, as worn by the luminous Karen Razler.

Suggested Uses

This is a good effect to use when casting a younger actor to play an older role, particularly in medium-size theaters.

It is also frequently used in television as an intermediate aging step when characters rapidly age over a few scenes, for example, the classic *Star Trek* episode in which the crew suddenly ages and the *X-Files* episode in which Mulder and Scully do the same.

Variations on this technique also work for large areas of scar tissue and a variety of burn and blister effects (see Chapter 4 for some alternate uses).

8
The Dead

Dead folks often put in an appearance onstage, particularly in the works of Shakespeare (Hamlet's father and Banquo's ghost, to name a few). Very often, they've died horrible deaths, which, for the makeup artist, makes it just that much more fun.

The makeup presented is not play-specific but a generic version of death showing the effects of a few weeks of interment. Depending on the overall concept of your production, you may require a more ghostly apparition, like the one presented in Chapter 9. This chapter's particular take on the dead walking among us is more zombielike than spectral.

For your particular design, with a specific character in mind, you'll want to dress the makeup with the appropriate costume and any wounds specific to the role. Hamlet's father, for example, might have blood or a noxious-looking poison stain seeping from one ear. Use this makeup as a springboard for your imagination, and see where it takes you.

Materials

To deck out your dead man walking, you will need

- ⊃ Liquid latex
- ⊃ Mortician's wax
- ⊃ Vaseline
- ⊃ Toilet paper, a few feet
- ⊃ Bruise wheel
- ⊃ Shadow wheel
- ⊃ Liquid foundation

- ➲ MagiColor Aqua Face Paints, accent colors
- ➲ Water
- ➲ Cataract effect contact lenses—optional, but cool
- ➲ Temporary tooth color or zombie teeth
- ➲ Food coloring
- ➲ Makeup sponges
- ➲ Assorted brushes
- ➲ Sculpting tool
- ➲ Scissors
- ➲ Hair dryer

The Makeup

As always, the actor's face should be clean. Since this makeup involves a lot of liquid latex, men should be freshly shaved. Women with that very faint, downy facial hair might want to wax or use a depilatory. The makeup will remove more easily (read: *painlessly*) after the fact if facial hair has been taken care of.

To begin, we're going to create that "been dead awhile" sunken-eye look.

1. Coat the actor's eyebrows with a very light coating of Vaseline. This will make removing the makeup easier.

2. Apply a coat of liquid latex over the actor's face.

3. Force dry the latex with a hair dryer.

4. Roll out several short lengths of mortician's wax, about one-quarter to one-half inch in diameter.

5. Begin building up the brow by blocking out the eyebrows with the mortician's wax.

6. Continue around the outside corner of each eye.

7. Complete the socket by adding wax under the eye, to the nose. You can see the rough shape of the eye sockets in Figure 8.1. It may take two or more layers of wax to achieve the look of depth you want.

8. Shape the wax and blend the edges into the skin using your fingers or a sculpting tool. A dab of Vaseline will keep the wax from sticking to either.

9. Blot excess Vaseline from the wax.

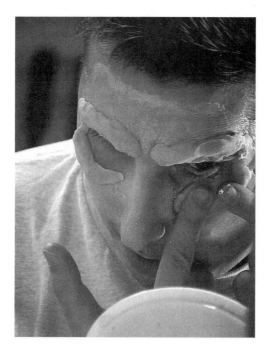

Figure 8.1   Create the sunken-eye look by building up the bones around the eye with mortician's wax.

10. Seal the mortician's wax with liquid latex.

11. Force dry using the dryer's cool setting.

12. Working in small sections, coat the wax in more latex, then apply the toilet tissue, covering both the inner and outer edges of the mortician's wax. Be *very* careful around the actor's eyes.

13. Plaster the tissue down with more latex. Don't worry about wrinkles or tears. The tissue adds the texture of dead skin—the nastier looking, the better.

14. Continue applying the toilet tissue to the actor's forehead, up to the hairline, and down the planes of both cheeks. Lay some on the bridge of the nose as well. You can see the application of the tissue in Figure 8.2.

15. Force dry the latex, still using the cool setting on the hair dryer.

16. Trim any extraneous tissue with small scissors.

17. Apply another coat of latex over all, particularly the edges.

18. Force it dry.

19. Powder the latex.

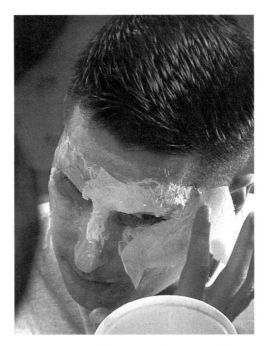

Figure 8.2   Working in small areas, apply
liquid latex, press on the tissue, then coat
again with latex.

> If you decide at this point that the eye sockets are not deep enough, you
> can still add more mortician's wax around the eyes. When you're done,
> simply seal with latex, force it dry, and apply another layer of tissue be-
> fore proceeding.

20. Make up the eyes with a medium brown from the Shadow wheel. This will
    accent the depth of the socket.

21. Using the same shade, lightly shadow the temples and the brow bone and
    hollow the cheeks. It doesn't have to be smooth and blended; we're going for
    a mottled effect here.

> This is the sort of makeup where forensic pathology textbooks come in
> very handy, particularly if you're going for a very realistic death effect.
> Just be prepared: the real images of death are *way* more upsetting than
> the FX makeup version.

22. Deepen the shadow areas using the purple from the Bruise wheel. Work purple into the edges of the shadows around the eye sockets as well. You want a mottled effect rather than a blended shadow.

23. From the shadow areas, trail off tendrils of color to simulate marbling. You can see what we mean in Figure 8.3.

24. Using the MagiColor Accent palette and a little water, mix a mossy green using the green and a touch of brown.

25. Use the mossy green color to lay in areas of mold.

26. Retouch and deepen shadow areas with the medium-brown crème color.

27. Mottle the face with a little more liquid foundation, paying extra attention to the highlight areas; it's acting as your highlight color. You can see a detail shot of the mottling effect in Figure 8.4.

28. Powder to set the makeup.

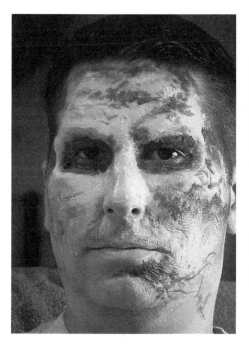

Figure 8.3   The mottled effect of the shadow, combined with the veinlike tendrils of purple, add to the look of decay.

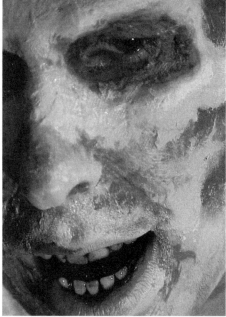

Figure 8.4   Detail shot of the mottled effect. This will be more helpful when used in conjunction with the final makeup shown in the color section of the book or with color images from the CD-ROM.

29. Add cataract contact lenses. These will impair the actor's vision. He'll be able to see, but through a milky fog.

30. Mix together a few drops of the four basic food colors, and have the actor swirl them around in his mouth. This will turn his tongue black, temporarily.

31. Put in a pair of zombie teeth (we show you how to make your own in Chapter 5) or discolor the actor's own teeth with temporary tooth stain or food coloring.

You can see the final makeup in Figure 8.5. We've added a little blood oozing from his mouth after a quick bite. You'll notice in the picture that the cataract contact lenses have a very subtle effect suitable for close-up photography and film, but—depending on the intimacy of your theater space—they probably aren't going to read well from a stage.

If you choose to go with effects lenses at all, you might want to go with a more dramatic pair—all white, all black, or even a florescent lens if your theater has black light.

Variations and Uses

As we mentioned at the beginning of the chapter, this is a non-character-specific take on the zombie that will work best if you tailor it to suit your production.

You can up the gross-out quotient by replacing the MagiColor moss with a moss-colored gelatin. Any cuts or wounds you might add can be dressed with a variety of bodily secretions from blood to pus. Chapter 6 contains a number of suitable recipes that can be adapted to your needs.

Figure 8.5   The final makeup, as worn by our model and makeup artist Dave Sartor.

9
Ghostly Visage

Intimations of death are everywhere in the theater. Shakespeare's body of work runs rampant with ghostly apparitions. There are a number of celebrated plays about haunted houses and haunted people in which the dead return to speak with the living—*A Shayna Maidel* comes to mind, as well as *Blithe Spirit*.

In some instances, it is appropriate to have a character, ghostly or not, appear with a somewhat dead look—victims of disease, holocaust survivors, and others who have been through extended periods of hardship.

The makeup presented here is a basic look of ghostlike death with an interesting twist. To accomplish it successfully, you will need the cooperation of a lighting designer adept at the subtle use of black light onstage—not an easy task.

The visible makeup is a nice, if simple, effect all by itself, but we're adding a subtle layer of fluorescent makeup that will imply the presence of (with apologies to P. D. James) the skull beneath the skin.

Materials

For this makeup, you will need

- ⊃ Fluorescent cake or crème makeup—it's colorless until hit with black light, and then it glows
- ⊃ Black light (available in most novelty stores, particularly around Halloween)
- ⊃ Shadow wheel
- ⊃ Bruise wheel
- ⊃ Clown White
- ⊃ Eyeliner

- ⊃ Translucent powder
- ⊃ Brushes
- ⊃ Makeup sponges
- ⊃ Black special-effects contact lenses (optional)

Fluorescent makeup is available from most theatrical makeup companies. In a pinch, you can get your hands on a bottle of the fluorescent ink they use to invisibly stamp the hands of patrons in most bars and dance clubs. It's available in novelty and some office supply stores. The ink is nontoxic and safe for use on skin and glows nicely under black light, but it tends to *linger* for a few days after application. That can be a lot of fun if you—or your actors—like to freak people out in the clubs.

The makeup and the ink are available in a number of different glow colors. For this effect, we've used a basic green. You can use whatever shade you like.

The Makeup

To begin, you'll need to work in a somewhat darkened room, at least until the first coat of fluorescent makeup has been applied. Plug in your black light and switch it on; you'll use it to check the application of makeup for the skull.

1. Lay in the rough shape of a skull on the actor's face using the fluorescent makeup, testing the application with the black light as shown in Figure 9.1.

> Getting this makeup to work effectively requires the participation of a good lighting designer in a controlled setting, because *any* extraneous light source hitting the makeup (other than the black light) will reduce the visibility of the glowing skull. It requires a facility that is capable of a nearly complete blackout. As you can see from the figures presented here, our workroom was not capable of such a blackout; while the effect worked, it was not pronounced enough to capture well on camera.

2. Shadow the actor's eyes with purple from the Bruise wheel, both the lids and below the eye, to give them a sunken appearance.

3. Shadow the planes of the cheeks for the drawn, gaunt look, following the natural lines of the face.

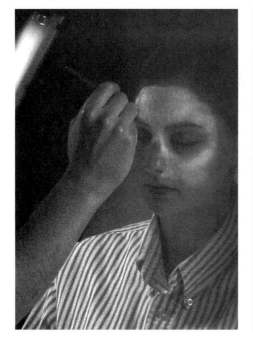

Figure 9.1   Using the black light to check your work, rough in the shape of a skull with the fluorescent makeup.

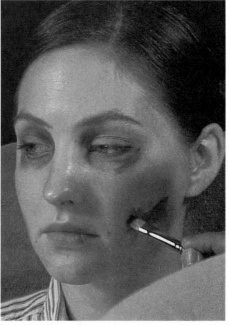

Figure 9.2   Shade the eyes and planes of the face and neck in purple from the Bruise wheel to give the actor's face that drawn, sunken look of death.

4. Shadow the temples. Blend back into the hairline.

5. Shadow the jawline, chin, mouth, and neck. On the neck, follow the lines of the tendons there, again to give that emaciated look. You can see the facial shadings in Figure 9.2.

6. Subtly blend the shadows into the skin with a sponge.

7. Using Clown White, apply highlights to the brow bone, nose, cheeks, chin, jaw, and neck to accentuate the shadows.

8. Blend the highlights with a makeup sponge.

9. Touch up shadows and highlights as necessary.

10. Powder to set.

11. Deepen the eye socket shading with a little black in the crease of the lid and below the eye.

12. Line the eyes with black eyeliner.

13. Add lip color, keeping in the purple/bruise range. You can see the completed *visible* makeup in Figure 9.3.

14. Retest the fluorescent makeup with the black light to see if the skull shape has survived the application of makeup.

15. Touch up the fluorescent makeup as necessary.

16. Powder to set.

17. Add the optional black contacts.

You can see the final makeup in Figure 9.4.

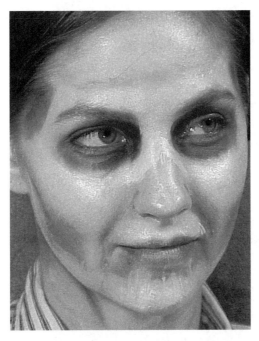

Figure 9.3   The visible portion of the makeup is a rather stylized image of death done in shades of purple on an otherwise pallid face.

You can increase the impact of the contact lenses by using fluorescent lenses, which can be acquired at one of the many special-effects lens companies. These lenses, however, are hand-painted and very expensive (as much as $500 per pair). You can create your own fluorescent lenses by tinting a pair of regular contact lenses with fluorescent ink. We don't recommend it, but it can be done. Soak the lenses in contact lens cleaning solution to which you've added four to five drops of all-natural, nontoxic fluorescent ink. Let them soak for an hour or two. Remove the lenses and rinse.

You can also change the color of plain lenses by tinting them with liquid, all-natural food or cake coloring.

Again, this is *not* recommended. We've both worn tinted lenses with no ill effect, but just because we're crazy enough to put them in *our* eyes doesn't mean you should be, too.

Figure 9.4   The final makeup, as worn by our model Susan Walton.

Suggested Uses

This makeup, with or without the glowing skull effect, is appropriate any time you have a ghostly apparition—Banquo's ghost (from the Scottish play), Hamlet's father, or any other ethereal character.

Toning down the stylized purple shadows, and making use of the blue-gray foundation color that bears the name of the play, gives you a good head start on the makeup for both ghosts in *Blithe Spirit*.

The glowing skull effect is not specifically called for in any play I'm aware of, it's just pretty darn cool and could, given the right production, be a startling capper to a dramatic moment, for example, when the Ghost of Christmas Yet to Come reveals his face. It would also be a lot of fun to use seasonally, for a haunted house, staged séance, or other Halloween-related production.

10
The Disfigured

There are a number of famous disfigured characters in the theater, probably the most famous being the Phantom of the Opera. Depending on the director's interpretation, Shakespeare's Richard III could be a good candidate as well.

Disfigurations, especially for principal roles, must be carefully planned out, keeping in mind the design considerations discussed back in Chapter 3. Particular attention must be paid to the permanence of the makeup and how it will affect the performance of the actor wearing it.

Michael Crawford, who originated the role of the Phantom, used to tell the story of how he had to be led around by stagehands backstage because the combination of the makeup and the famous mask that covered it almost completely obliterated his vision.

The makeup we've done for you here is an excellent disfiguring burn, whether from acid (a la the movie interpretation of *Phantom of the Opera*), accident, or fire. It is reasonably permanent and designed to have a minimal impact on the actor's performance. However, because the disfiguration involves the use of a special contact lens in one eye, the actor's depth perception could be affected.

This effect uses an industrial-strength gelatin to achieve the disfiguration. It would be most effective for a limited-run production, on a character with limited stage time or intermittent scenes that would allow for touchups to the makeup. For longer runs or characters with almost constant stage time, it would probably be more cost-effective to go with foam latex appliances, if you have the time, equipment, and budget to construct your own or have them built for you.

Materials

The supplies you'll need to complete this makeup include

- ➲ 6 packets of unflavored gelatin (Knox works best)
- ➲ Water
- ➲ Small saucepan
- ➲ Hot plate or stove
- ➲ Liquid latex
- ➲ Burn wheel
- ➲ Dry foundation cake
- ➲ Liquid foundation
- ➲ Roll of toilet paper or box of facial tissue
- ➲ Hair dryer
- ➲ Stage blood
- ➲ Effects gel blood or Fresh Scab Gel
- ➲ Dish soap
- ➲ K-Y Jelly or hairstyling gel
- ➲ Cataract contact lens
- ➲ Makeup sponges
- ➲ Assortment of brushes

Preparation

Before you get your actor in the chair, you need to prepare the gelatin. This is one of those annoying "by eye" concoctions for which there's no real recipe, since factors like humidity, the amount of heat applied, and the quality of the gelatin you use all affect the final product. The general proportions, however, are about one cup of water for every three packs of unflavored gelatin.

For this makeup, we prepared six packets of gelatin—much more than needed for the effect. As always, it's better to have too much than not enough.

This gelatin mixture freezes well. Cool any leftover gelatin and let it solidify in the saucepan. Peel it out of the pan, slap it into a zippered freezer bag, and freeze it. When you want to reuse it, you can either reheat it by itself, adding a few drops of water at a time until it returns to the proper consistency, or add the recycled gelatin to a new batch, adjusting the water content as necessary.

Bring one cup of water to a boil. Add the gelatin and stir until the gelatin is melted. The gelatin will thicken up quickly, so keep the second cup handy to add more as you go. Add only a little water at a time. You're creating what the science types call a supersaturated solution.

When the gelatin is melted, let it simmer and stir frequently until the mixture thickens to about the consistency of dish soap while hot. Then remove it from the heat and let it cool a little.

As the gelatin cools, it will thicken, so you'll need to work fairly fast or be prepared to reheat the gelatin along the way.

You can pour some of the gelatin into a bowl, to work with immediately, and leave the rest in the pot on a low heat to keep it liquid, then just trade off as the gelatin in the bowl sets.

A double boiler is handy to keep the gelatin warm and liquid without overcooking or burning it. However, you have to do the initial gelatin preparation in a pan on a direct flame. A double boiler just doesn't get hot enough to cook the gelatin.

The Makeup

Once the gelatin is prepared, you're ready to disfigure. Wrap your actor in a towel or other coverup; the gelatin can be a little drippy. To begin:

1. Coat the area of the actor's face to be disfigured with a thin coat of liquid latex.

2. Let the latex dry or force dry it with a hair dryer.

3. Paint on a coat of gelatin using a wide paint brush.

4. Begin to apply toilet tissue, as you would papier-mâché: dip 4- to 6-inch lengths of tissue in the gelatin, squeeze out excess gelatin, and apply tissue to the face, as shown in Figure 10.1.

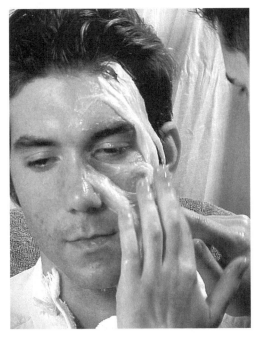

Figure 10.1 Apply the gelatin-soaked tissue to simulate exposed face muscles and ruined flesh.

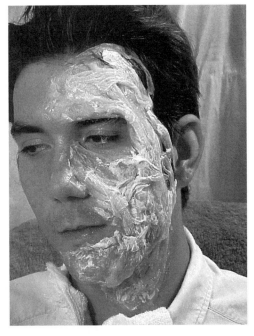

Figure 10.2 You can sculpt the tissue with a sculpting tool or the end of a brush to suggest exposed muscles and flaps of skin.

5. Sculpt and shape the tissue to suggest exposed face muscles and ruined flesh. Work in thin layers to facilitate drying, and build up. You can see the sculpted tissue in Figure 10.2.

6. Force dry the tissue. The gelatin sets from the outside in, so you'll want to make sure it's dried through.

7. When the gelatin is dry, coat the tissue with a thin layer of latex to seal it. Be sure to get in all the little grooves and crevasses.

8. Force dry the latex.

9. Using your Burn wheel, lay the lightest shade of red into the pockets and hollows of the tissue, as shown in Figure 10.3.

10. Powder using the dry foundation cake; it adds a little extra flesh color to the disfiguration.

11. Sponge a sallow, liquid foundation on the raised areas of tissue.

12. Touch up shadow color.

95

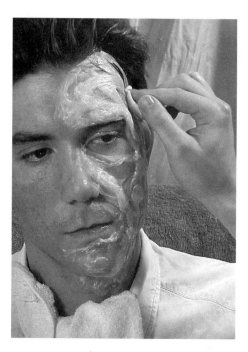

Figure 10.3 Using the lightest shade from the Burn wheel, apply color to the pockets and creases of tissue. Powder using a dry foundation cake.

13. In the pockets and creases, lay in the darker red from the Burn wheel, keeping to the lower edges of the pockets. It will pop the color of the burn, as well as accent the dimensionality of the makeup.

14. Make up around the eye with the midtones from the Burn wheel to give it that deeply socketed look.

15. Apply the deepest red from the Burn wheel and slight touches of black to increase the crispiness of the look.

16. Blend all edges, particularly into the actor's hairline and un-madeup skin.

17. Powder to set.

18. Add cataract contact lens to disfigured eye. You can see this stage of the makeup in Figure 10.4.

At this point, you have an effective, recently healed disfiguration. To take it a step further and make it a fresh injury, we're going to lay in some stage blood.

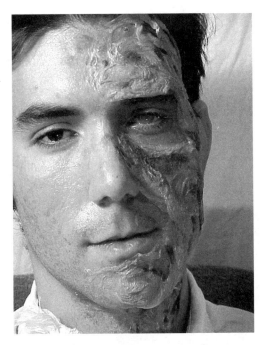

Figure 10.4   After applying the principal
burn colors, add the cataract contact lens to
the disfigured eye.

19. Dress burns with liquid stage blood to which you've added a drop or two of
    liquid dish soap. The soap keeps the blood from beading up on the latex and
    oil-based makeup.

20. Around the eye, use an Effects gel blood, or Fresh Scab Gel; the thicker con-
    sistency keeps the blood from running into the actor's eye.

21. Using hair gel or K-Y Jelly, grease up the actor's hair around the injury for
    that stringy, bloody look.

> You can make your own gel blood by mixing a little regular stage blood
> with K-Y Jelly. You can even make your own blood, if you'd like. Chap-
> ter 6 includes blood recipes, as well as recipes for other bodily fluids.

You can see the finished makeup in Figure 10.5. It's a startling effect, particularly
with the white cataract staring out of the bloody, ruined flesh.

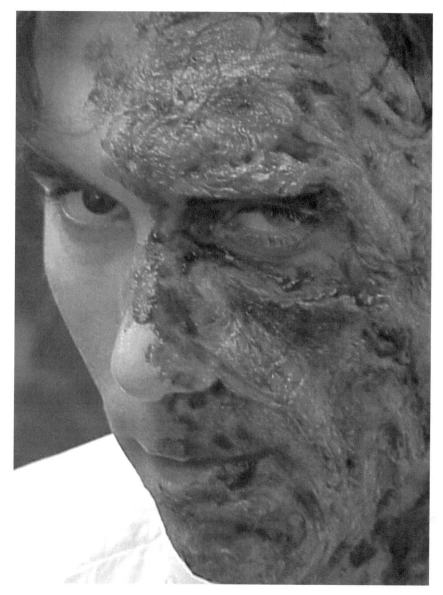

Figure 10.5   The final makeup, as worn by our model John Yeomans.

Variations

This is a fairly versatile makeup that can give you the full range of the process of healing. As shown in Figure 10.5, you have a very recent disfigurement. Left as shown in Figure 10.4, you have a recently healed injury. Change the color palette away from the red range and back to more normal skin tones highlighted with scar-tissue white, and you'll have a long-healed injury.

11
Crash/Beating Victim

$\mathcal{T}$here is a rich history in the theater of beating the crap out of the occasional character, particularly in plays like *Golden Boy* and *The Great White Hope*.

Depending on the play and the timing of the beating victim's appearance, you may only have time to dress up your actor using your Bruise wheel and some blood (as described in Chapters 4 and 6, respectively).

However, if you have a little time to prepare the actor's face for a full-fledged, "buddy you look like you got run over by a truck" makeup, combining those bruise effects with some dimensional makeup can really heighten the effect.

For this makeup, we've chosen to simulate the effects of a serious beating, concentrating mainly on the eye and nose—the points that tend to take it on the chin, as it were, in any fistfight. Using primarily mortician's wax and your Bruise wheel, you'll create an eye that's been swollen shut by a good right hook. It also works for an automobile accident.

A Note of Caution

You'll be working directly over the actor's eye for much of this makeup, sculpting and then dressing the mortician's wax with makeup to create the swollen eyelid. As always, when working on or around an actor's eyes, exercise caution.

Also, you'll notice that there's a distinct lack of adhesives in the upcoming list of materials. This makeup is designed to be short-lived, for two reasons.

First, the beating victim often makes a return appearance shortly after the beating. You need to be able to quickly remove the dimensional makeup and recolor the bruises to give the appearance that the victim is healing.

Second, adhesives are always dicey around the eyes. Liquid latex, for example, frequently contains ammonia, which is an eye irritant. If you must get a more durable effect for your production, you'll want to carefully apply an adhesive around the perimeter of the eye before you apply the mortician's wax. You might even want to consider using a foam latex appliance instead of the wax.

Materials

To accomplish this effect, you're going to need the following:

- Mortician's wax
- Bruise wheel
- Shadow wheel
- Highlight wheel
- Blood or gel blood
- Liquid tooth color, black
- Translucent powder
- Vaseline
- Cotton balls or dentist's spit pads
- Sculpting tool
- Brushes
- Sponges

Preparation

You can save some wear and tear on the actor's eye by doing a little presculpting. Rough out the shape of the swollen eye in mortician's wax. Make the piece large enough to fill the actor's eye socket, even a little larger—about the size of a hard-boiled egg cut in half lengthwise. You can always trim away any excess during the application process. Using the sculpting tool, etch in the split between the two lids.

Set it aside until you're ready to apply it.

The Makeup

To begin, we're going to break the actor's nose a little.

1. Apply a ball of mortician's wax at the side of the bridge of the actor's nose, to give the appearance of a broken nose.

2. Shape and sculpt the wax using the sculpting tool, blending the edges of the wax into the actor's skin.

3. Apply the preformed eye piece over the actor's eye, pressing it firmly into place. You can see the positioning and rough shape of the swollen eye in Figure 11.1.

Most makeup artists get a little nervous when they work around an actor's eye like this. It might help you if you allow the actor himself to do the pressing into place of the mortician's wax. That way, the actor gets to be a part of the process, and you don't have to worry about pressing too hard and hurting him.

4. Blend the edges of the wax eye into the surrounding skin and up to the brow bone.

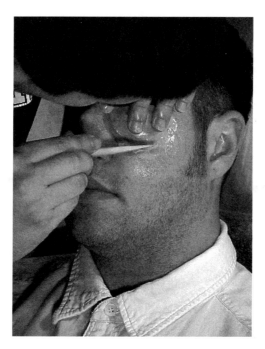

Figure 11.1   Place the preformed swollen eye over the actor's eye and press it firmly into place, then blend the edges into the skin and brow as shown.

5. If necessary, apply additional mortician's wax to the upper lid to exaggerate the swelling. Blend into the original piece.

6. Resculpt the overall shape as necessary, and reinforce the crease between the lids. Use the sculpting tool to get a good solid line.

7. With a brush, begin laying in the deep purple bruise color from the Bruise wheel around the mortician's wax on the nose and eye. Be sure to cover the joint between the skin and the wax. Because fresh bruises tend to appear more mottled, dab the color on rather than using longer brush strokes.

8. Take the bruise color up the actor's forehead, above the swollen eye, and down the plane of his cheek below the eye.

9. Extend the bruise color for the nose out below the undamaged eye; broken noses tend to bruise along the soft tissues of the sinus areas, almost in a butterfly shape. You can see the full set of bruises in Figure 11.2.

10. Blend the outer edges of the bruises into the surrounding skin, keeping the darkest shading near the mortician's wax.

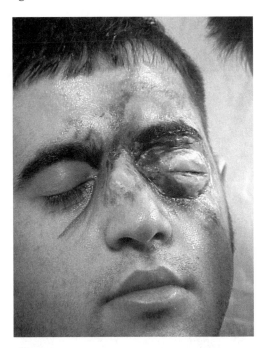

Figure 11.2   The mottled bruises should extend out beyond the damaged eye and broken nose. Bruises resulting from a broken nose tend to follow along the sinus area, both above and below the eye.

11. Apply a yellow bruise highlight to the swollen lid and broken nose areas. Work a little into the surrounding bruise areas to increase the mottling effect.

12. Powder to set the bruises.

13. Dress the broken nose with a little stage blood or an effects gel blood.

14. Add a little blood near the corner of the mouth, as if the actor's lip had been split in the fight. The applied blood is shown in Figure 11.3.

You can get a nice-looking cut by applying the blood or effects gel with the flat end of the sculpting tool; it lays on the blood like a palette knife, giving you the same crisp, clean line that a cut would have.

15. Knock out a few of the actor's teeth by blacking them out with temporary tooth stain. Dry the actor's teeth first using tissue or a paper towel to improve the stain's adhesion, then brush on the stain. Let it dry.

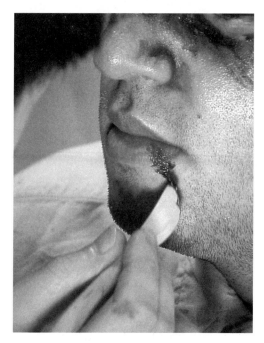

Figure 11.3 The addition of a little effects gel blood to the broken nose and lip add to the realism of the effect.

16. Stuff the sides of the actor's mouth with cotton balls or a few of those spit pads dentists use during procedures. It generally increases the swollen look of the actor's face.

17. Retouch makeup as necessary.

You can see the effects of our virtual beating in Figure 11.4. To give him the look of a boxer who has been beaten in the ring, we smeared the swollen eye with Vaseline, the ringside treatment of choice to quickly stop bleeding. This may or may not be appropriate for your beating victim.

Variations

There are many possible variations on this makeup. Given the time, the tools, and the inclination, you can bruise, bend, break, or otherwise mutilate any facial feature to accommodate the needs of your particular production. For a car wreck victim, for example, you might want to substitute a hematoma on the forehead for the swollen eye.

The injuries shown here are realistic. For comedies and lighter fare, you might want to soften the effect by eliminating the blood and easing up on the bruises. When doing trauma effects for nondramas, I always find it best to keep them at a cartoon level—literally. Think of the injuries your average Warner Brothers cartoon character survives, bloodlessly. When the effect gets too realistic, it stops being funny.

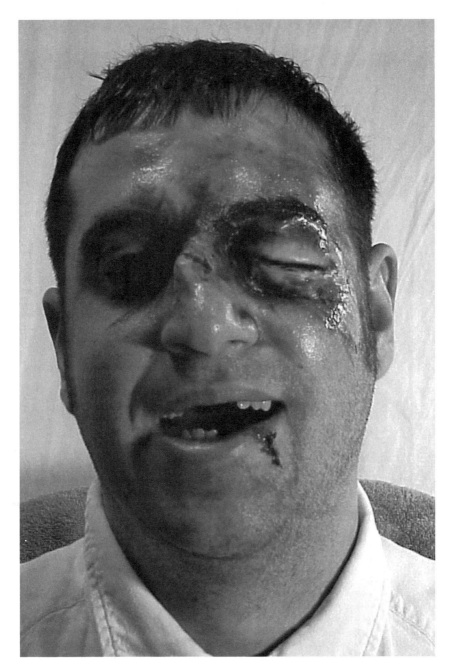

Figure 11.4   The final beating, as worn by our model Matt Harchick.

12
Gouged Eyes

The gouged eye effect demonstrated here is rather graphic and grue-some—in other words, very *cool*. It gives the actor the appearance of having had his or her eyes gouged out, without major vision impairment (if the actor can squint well). The effect is an elaboration of the "Build-a-Scar 101" section of Chapter 5, so if you haven't read that, you might want to flip back there for a quick look.

The appliances used are built by hand for this effect. For an extended run, you might want to consider casting these appliances in foam or slush latex.

This effect will come in handy for productions of *Oedipus* and also for the odd zom-bie, mutilated demon, or other minion of the netherworld. It's also just generally creepy-looking.

Materials

To execute this makeup, you will need the following supplies:

- ➲ Pane of glass
- ➲ Liquid latex
- ➲ Facial tissue
- ➲ Hair dryer
- ➲ Brushes
- ➲ Sponges
- ➲ Pros-Aide
- ➲ Adhesive Blending Paste
- ➲ Greasepaint, flesh palette
- ➲ Greasepaint, black

⮑ Stage blood

⮑ Thick blood

⮑ Scissors

⮑ Precision knife or safety razor

⮑ Sculpting tool

⮑ Hair dryer

⮑ Translucent powder

⮑ Press powder, black

Preparation

This particular makeup is all about preparation. The construction of the gouged eye appliances should happen well in advance of getting your actor in the chair. It will help if you have rough measurements of the actor's eyes—even a rough tracing on paper—to place under the glass as you construct the appliances.

To create these appliances, follow the steps below:

1. Working on a clean sheet of glass (approximately 10″ × 12″), apply a coating of liquid latex to the glass slightly larger than size of the final appliances. Leave an uncovered space for each of the eye sockets.

2. Force dry.

3. Repeat steps 1 and 2.

4. After the second coat of latex has dried, begin building up the fake eyelids with tissue. Apply another coat of the latex over the dry latex. Lay on tissue, and coat the tissue with latex. While the tissue is wet, begin roughing out the shape of the upper and lower lids. You can see the sculpting process in Figure 12.1.

5. Force dry.

6. Repeat steps 4 and 5, as necessary, building up the lid area to approximate the gaping hole that would be left by the removal of someone's eyeballs. You can see the final shape of our appliances in Figure 12.2.

> For an extra touch of realism, you can add false eyelashes to the appliances, like those used in the Male-to-Female Drag makeup in Chapter 15.

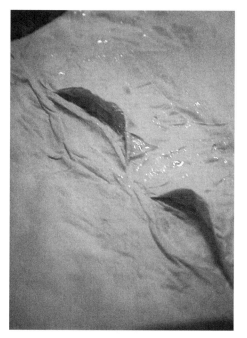
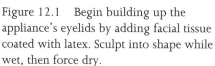
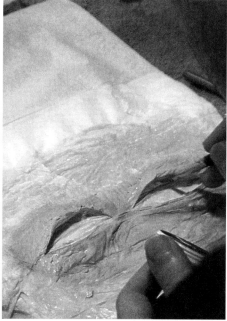

Figure 12.1   Begin building up the appliance's eyelids by adding facial tissue coated with latex. Sculpt into shape while wet, then force dry.

Figure 12.2   Repeat the tissue/latex application until your ruined eyes take on the shape you want.

7. Let the appliances dry well, at least overnight. You can tell if they've truly dried through by looking at the underside of the glass—you'll see if the interior latex is still wet or not.

8. When dry, prepare to remove the appliances from the glass by gently dusting them with translucent powder.

9. Carefully ease the edge of a safety razor or precision knife under the edge of the appliance and lift. You don't want to cut the appliance, just loosen a little of it from the glass.

10. Dust a little powder under the edge of the appliance to prevent it from sticking to itself.

11. Gently peel a little more from the glass.

12. Repeat steps 10 and 11 until the appliance is free from the glass.

13. You can, if you care to, make up the appliances in advance, using greasepaint, rubber mask grease, or PAX Paint.

14. Powder the makeup to set, or let the PAX Paint dry, and you're ready for your actor.

PAX Paint is a permanent appliance paint made by tinting Pros-Aide with acrylic paint or greasepaint. You can then paint the appliances with the PAX Paint and let it dry. You can do a complete makeup on latex and gel appliances using PAX Paint, then simply use makeup to get the actor's skin to match, once the appliance is on.

The Makeup

Once you have the actor in the chair, you're ready to trim and fit the appliances.

1. Place the appliances over the actor's eyes and check placement and size.

2. If necessary, trim the appliances to size. You want to leave a narrow margin of excess latex around the appliances as a blending edge. You can see our appliances, trimmed to fit, in Figure 12.3. For ease of fitting them in place, we wound up with four pieces—two upper lids and two lower lids—trimmed to fit together precisely.

3. When the appliances are trimmed, carefully brush Pros-Aide around the actor's eye, let it set up a moment, then apply the first latex piece. Hold it in place, or have the actor hold it, until the Pros-Aide dries.

4. Repeat until all the appliance pieces are in place. You can see the placement of the pieces in Figure 12.4.

5. Use a little Adhesive Blending Paste and a wet cotton swab or makeup sponge to smooth the seams between the appliances and the actor's skin.

6. Let the molding paste dry, or force it dry with a hair dryer.

7. Once the molding paste dries, you can complete the actor's makeup. For this demonstration, we've done just a very basic makeup, but you can work this effect into any design. The key element is to make sure you blacken the actor's eyelids with greasepaint, so that when his eyes are closed (he can squint, if necessary, to see), it looks like he has great gaping holes where his eyes should be. Powder the greasepaint with black press powder to set.

 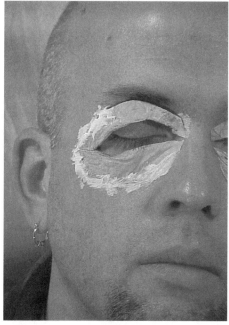

Figure 12.3   Try the appliances on for size, then trim to fit, leaving a thin blending edge around the appliance pieces.

Figure 12.4   Attach the appliances with Pros-Aide and mask the seams with a little Adhesive Blending Paste.

> You could also build the appliances as two pieces, one for each eye, and line the eye opening with a black, scrimlike material that would further intensify the effect.

8. For that freshly gouged look, dress the appliances with a little gel blood around the eye sockets.

9. Dribble a little stage blood from the eyes so that it runs down the actor's face. You can see the final effect in Figure 12.5.

Suggested Uses

As mentioned at the beginning of the chapter, this effect is excellent for Oedipus, but it has applications anywhere you need, well, one or more gouged-out eyes. It's a good zombie and demon effect, as well, and can be easily worked into any makeup design. Imagination is your only limitation.

Figure 12.5   The final gouged eye effect, as worn by model John Pivovarnick.

The Thing makeup, as worn by model David Sartor.
Multiple layers of color give the makeup depth, while the
goat-like lenses and vulpine teeth finish the effect.

The Dead, as modeled by Dave Sartor, combines both dimensional and paint techniques to create a flesh-hungry ghoul.

The Thing makeup, as worn by model David Sartor.
Multiple layers of color give the makeup depth, while the
goat-like lenses and vulpine teeth finish the effect.

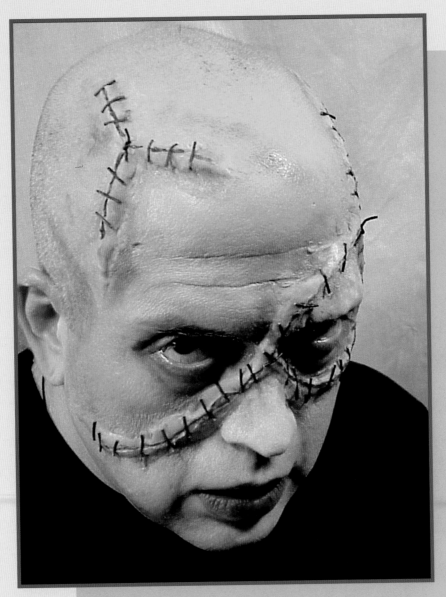

Our take on Frankenstein's creature is actually a fairly simple combination of paint and mortician's wax. The single cataract contact lens adds to the assembled feeling.

An elegant Elizabethan makeup, as worn by model Phoebe Sharp, that with minor adjustment, is appropriate for a century's worthy of courtly women—and some men.

The Beast/Wolf Man makeup, as worn by model John
Pivovarnick, can easily be adapted for a number of beastly,
Neanderthal-like characters.

The Disfigured, modeled by John Yeomans, is a flexible effect that can be used to simulate a recent burn injury, or long-healed scar tissue.

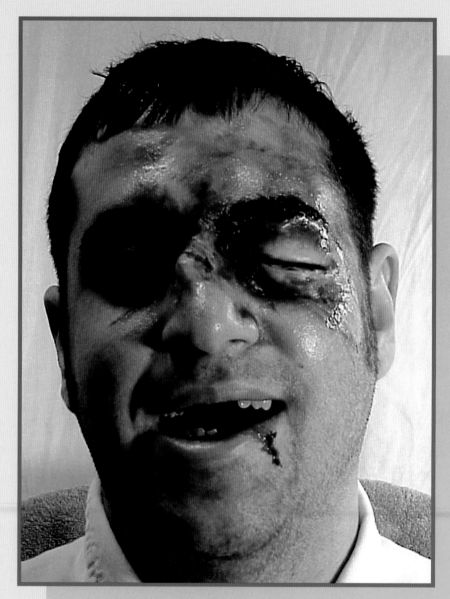

The final beating, as worn by model Matt Harchick, employs a subtle use of dimensional makeup that can be easily removed for a quick, on-stage recovery.

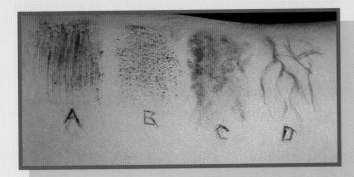

Four basic methods for laying paint on skin using a stipple sponge or brush, as discussed in Chapter 5.

Four basic blending techniques, labeled E through H, also described in Chapter 5.

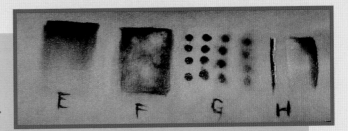

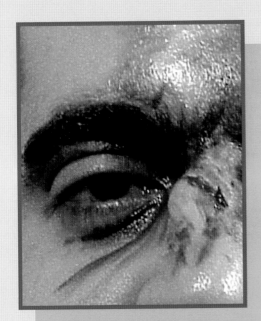

A natural-looking bruise combines both mottling and blending techniques. Modeled by Matt Harchick

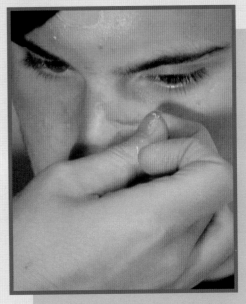

A sunburn effect is as simple as a coating of latex followed by a red foundation, with some latex peeled and pulled to form blisters and flaps of skin. Modeled by John Imblis

The Dead, as modeled by Dave Sartor, combines both dimensional and paint techniques to create a flesh-hungry ghoul.

13
Leprosy

Leprosy, also known as Hanson's disease, is a common affliction in many religious pageants and theatrical productions; sometimes the lepers even get to sing and dance, as in the case of *Jesus Christ Superstar*.

Leprosy is a horribly disfiguring disease that has centuries of fear and prejudice associated with it. Very often, the makeup for a leper is complicated by the fact that it must be quickly and easily removed onstage. In most religious pageants, the leper(s) get cured by a miracle.

To that end, the makeup that follows is an extreme case of leprosy that has the advantage of being easily removed to effect the miraculous cure. As such, it is appropriate only for short-term use and not at all appropriate for a strenuous or quick-change role, like the lepers in *Superstar*.

> For a more lasting effect, you might want to build appliances out of latex, as described in Chapter 5. If you have the time, the equipment, and/or the budget, you might also want to consider casting appliances out of foam latex or foaming gelatin.

This makeup was based on information found at a number of leprosy/Hanson's disease information sites scattered about the Internet, which is an excellent source of information, if you have the time and patience to sift through all of the information available there.

Materials

To execute this makeup, you will need the following supplies:

- Liquid latex
- Unflavored gelatin (Knox is preferred)
- Toilet paper
- Liquid foundation in an appropriate shade
- Cake foundation in an appropriate shade
- Greasepaint or rubber mask grease, flesh-tone palette
- Shadow wheel
- Highlight wheel
- Translucent powder
- Vaseline
- Hair dryer
- Brushes
- Makeup sponges
- Hair clip or elastic, to get the actor's hair out of the way, if necessary

Preparation

This makeup uses the same gelatin concoction used for the disfiguration in Chapter 10. Before you get your actor in the chair, it's best to have the gelatin cooked and cooled to the point where it can be safely applied to the actor's face.

The only difference between the gelatin mixture used in Chapter 10 and the one used here is that we've pretinted the gelatin by mixing in color cake foundation of an appropriate shade by scraping foundation from the round into the hot gelatin mixture and stirring. This gives you a little less work to do after the makeup is applied, since you don't have to struggle to get foundation color into all of the nooks and crannies of the makeup.

You'll also find it will save some time and aggravation if you prepare about fifteen to twenty short lengths of toilet tissue (two to four squares each) beforehand. While working with the gelatin, your fingers tend to get very sticky, and wrestling tissue from the roll can be quite irritating.

You will also find it handy to have a few extra towels or moist towelettes around to keep your fingers clear of gelatin buildup. We like to use cloth towels, which you can wet and then microwave for about thirty to forty seconds, depending on the strength of your microwave oven. Try short time periods and increase until the towel is bearably hot to the touch—you *don't* want to burn yourself.

Microwaving a moist towel gives you an old-fashioned hot towel, which almost instantly dissolves the accumulated gelatin on your hands. If you don't have access to a microwave, wash your hands frequently in warm soapy water. You can also give your hands a quick, light coat of Vaseline before you begin to prevent sticking.

The Makeup

With the prep work out of the way, you're ready to begin.

1. Clip or pull the actor's hair out of the way, if necessary, before you begin.

2. Coat the actor's face with a thin layer of liquid latex.

3. Air or force dry.

4. Brush on a thin coating of your prepared gelatin; test the temperature first.

5. Begin building the leprous growths with short lengths of toilet tissue dipped in the gelatin mixture. Remember to squeeze the excess gelatin from the tissue first. Take time to force dry regularly. You don't want to wait too long between drying sessions, or the gelatin will take much longer to set up on the actor's face. You can see the beginning of the application process in Figure 13.1.

6. You may work in any order you care to, but these are the areas we built up, in the order we built them:
   - Cheek bones
   - Chin
   - Nose
   - Brow bone and forehead

7. Once the growths have been built and sculpted into shape, brush a coating of gelatin over all. You can see the finished application of growths in Figure 13.2.

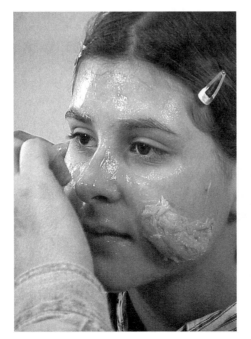

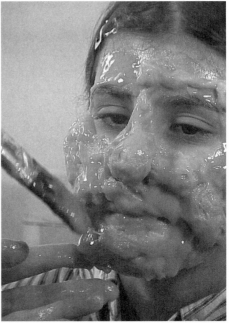

Figure 13.1   After coating the actor's face with a layer of latex and your gelatin mixture, begin to build up the leprous growths with gelatin-soaked tissue.

Figure 13.2   Before the gelatin sets, the tissue can be easily sculpted to resemble late-stage leprosy.

8. Force dry.

9. Powder to absorb any residual surface moisture.

10. Make up exposed areas of skin with foundation to match the tinted gelatin.

11. Using the Shadow wheel, accent the shadow areas of the growths—crevasses and hollows.

12. Sponge on liquid foundation or rubber mask grease over all, particularly prominences and exposed skin. Use a shade one or two steps lighter than the gelatin color.

13. Sponge on subtle highlight color. You can see the layered appearance this gives to the makeup in Figure 13.3.

14. Apply eyebrow pencil to any visible eyebrow.

15. Make up eyes in neutral/natural tones.

Figure 13.3   The combination of the tinted gelatin, the foundation color, and the applied shadows and highlights gives a very natural, layered look to the makeup.

16. If necessary, touch up the makeup, being sure to blend into the hairline and around the eyes, neck, ears, and so on.

17. Style the actor's hair—or unstyle it, as the case may be. You can see the final makeup in Figure 13.4.

Suggested Uses

As mentioned at the beginning of the chapter, this is not an appropriate makeup to use for a physically demanding role. It is, however, ideal to use for short stage appearances, film work (where you have a lot of time available for retouching), and especially for roles in which the leper is miraculously cured of his or her affliction.

The makeup can be easily removed onstage to effect the miracle; simply peel it away. The tinting of the gelatin minimizes the risk of exposing the trick. Since the

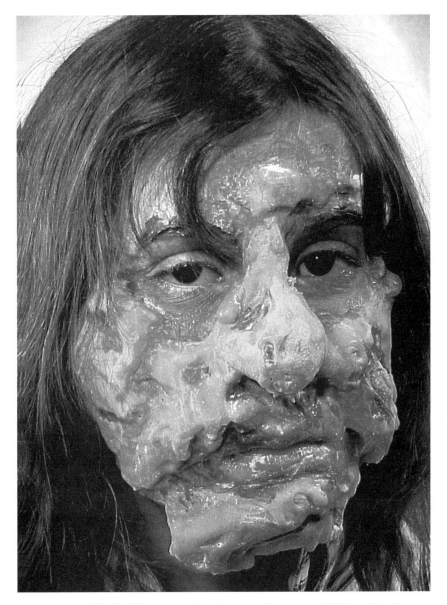

Figure 13.4   The final leprosy makeup, as worn by our model Sierra Lancia.

saturated toilet tissue is all tinted with foundation color, there is little risk of exposing brilliant white tissue within the makeup.

Gelatin is a very versatile tool in the effects makeup artist's bag of tricks, and this technique can be easily adapted to create multiple effects.

14
Crossing Ethnic Lines

Depending on the ethnic composition of the city in which you work and live, you may find yourself in the position of having to make up an actor of one ethnic background to allow him or her to portray someone of another ethnic background; particularly with many of the multicultural/diversity pieces written for children's theater.

It's a difficult task for the makeup artist, because you have to come up with a makeup that satisfies the needs of the play, helps the actor develop the role, and remains true to the culture you're trying to capture in makeup. Your best preparation is a healthy dose of research, adding information and photographs to your photo morgue as described in Chapter 2.

For this example, we chose to turn a Caucasian girl into an Indian girl. Since we were not working with a particular script in mind, we did a minimal amount of research. Had the script required it, though, we would have researched the relevant details of social and caste status in India and worked with the actress, the costume designer, and the director to establish the exact look required by the production.

Materials

For this makeup, you will need

- ꙮ Bronzing Body Tint
- ꙮ Makeup sponges
- ꙮ Shadow and Highlight wheels
- ꙮ Black eyeliner, liquid or pencil

➲ Black mascara

➲ Red and yellow crème colors

➲ Appropriate lip color

Depending on whom you're making up, you might also need to apply a temporary hair color—in this case, dark brown or black—to the actor's hair. Our model already had dark brown hair, so we didn't mess with it.

The Makeup

We chose to use Ben Nye's Bronzing Body Tint rather than a traditional foundation simply because it looks better; because it's a transparent liquid, the actor's skin looks natural, rather than like a thick coat of spackle. Be sure to use the body tint in a well-ventilated area. The fumes can be a bit much in a confined, airless space.

To begin:

1. Apply the Bronzing Body Tint to the actor's face, ears, and other areas of exposed skin using a makeup sponge. Don't forget to work it into the hairline, too.

2. You will notice that the tint tends to streak when wet. You can see what I mean in Figure 14.1. Let the Bronzing Body Tint dry a bit, then smooth out the coverage with a clean sponge or your hands. It washes off with soap and water.

3. When the first coat is dry, apply additional coats, as above, until you reach the desired skin tone. For our model, it took about five coats.

4. Using the black eyeliner, heavily line the eyes. Fully line the upper lid. On the lower lid, start at about the center and line out beyond the corner of the eye, as shown in Figure 14.2.

5. Make up the eyes as you would for someone who is not supposed to be wearing eye makeup; stick to natural shadow and highlight colors.

6. Apply natural lip color.

7. Contour the cheeks with a natural rouge.

8. Use a deep red crème color to apply the third-eye spot, centered just above the eyebrows. You can see the positioning in Figure 14.3.

If you were going for an everyday look, the makeup would end here. However, we chose to take it a step further. For certain ceremonial and cultural occasions,

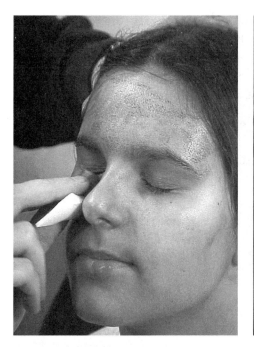

Figure 14.1   The Bronzing Body Tint tends to streak when wet. You can even it out when it begins to dry by using a clean sponge or your hands.

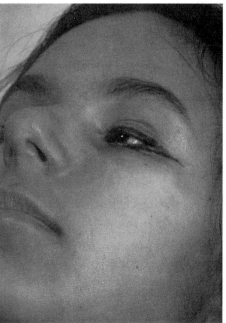

Figure 14.2   The eyes should be heavily lined in black, and the lower lid line should extend out beyond the corner of the eye.

Figure 14.3   The third-eye spot should be centered between the eyebrows and a little bit above.

Hindu women often work a little red powder (like a rouge) into the part of their hair and add additional decorative touches to the makeup.

9. For the red, we worked a little red crème foundation into the part of our model's hair and extended the line about an inch down her forehead.

10. Finally, we circled the red with bright yellow and added a row of dots in the same crème yellow on either side of her forehead, just above the eyebrows.

11. Powder to set makeup. The Bronzing Body Tint doesn't require powder to set, just the crème colors do.

You can see the final makeup in Figure 14.4. Of course, for full effect, the actress would need to be costumed in a sari, with jewelry and accessories as required.

Suggested Uses

Bronzing Body Tint can be used any time you need to darken and/or tan an actor's skin, whatever his or her original skin tone. As you can imagine, it's used heavily on *Baywatch* and can add another touch of realism to plays set in the summer and performed in winter.

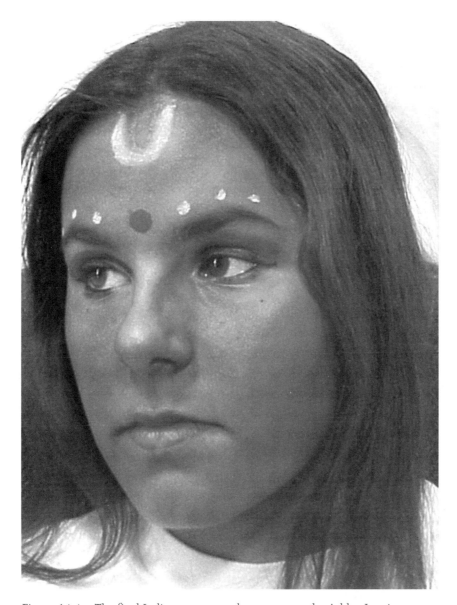

Figure 14.4   The final Indian woman makeup, as worn by Ashley Lancia.

15
Drag

Gender-bending for the stage has been around, well, probably as long as there have been stages; any theater history text will tell you how a life in the theater was second only to prostitution as a low-life career choice, especially for women.

Given that, most classical roles written for women and girls were actually played by men and young boys, particularly in Shakespeare's time.

Nowadays, of course, there's no such bias against women in the theater; however, the occasional need for a drag transformation still arises in modern productions. *Chicago, Greater Tuna, M Butterfly,* and *La Cage aux Folles* all require cross-dressing in one direction or another.

In other productions, while not required, it may solve difficult casting choices. For a production of *The Importance of Being Earnest*, a director friend was nearly left without a sufficiently imposing Lady Bracknell; until the right actress walked in, he was all set to cast a 6'3" 270-pound man in the role.

This chapter drags you in both directions—male to female and female to male. The makeup designs presented here are for realistic transformations, as opposed to the more highly stylized drag favored by drag performers. Drag-queen drag is an art form unto itself.

Male-to-Female Drag

Turning a man into a woman is probably the most common drag transformation. It will require an item or two that you might not have handy in your makeup kit, such as falsies and false eyelashes.

Additionally, to be truly effective, you'll need the appropriate costume and accessories to complete the illusion. You'll need to work closely with the costume designer and the director to get the exact look you need.

If the actor will be required to wear high-heeled shoes, it's best to get him a pair for rehearsals in addition to the pair for the costume; they take some getting used to, especially for someone who's worn flats all his life. This isn't really the responsibility of the makeup artist, but it's something to keep in mind for the sake of the actor and his ankles.

Materials

In order to execute this design, you will need

- Mellow Yellow
- 5 O' Sharp, if necessary to cover a beard shadow
- Crème or liquid foundation in an appropriate shade
- Lip color
- Lip liner
- Blush
- Eye shadow
- Eyeliner
- Mascara
- Eyebrow pencil
- False eyelashes (the individual kind, not the full fake lashes) and adhesive
- Wig
- Tweezers
- Sponges
- Brushes

We're going for a streetwear look, so the choice of lip, eye, and blush colors is completely up to you and your actor's wardrobe and skin tone.

The Makeup

Before you begin, you should make sure that your actor's face is both freshly washed and closely shaved.

1. If necessary, apply Mellow Yellow to any blemishes and 5 O' Sharp to any beard shadow. Our model had some acne that we masked with Mellow Yellow. You can see the blemishes disappear in Figure 15.1.

> Coverups like Mellow Yellow work by covering discolorations with a neutralizing color. Mellow Yellow mutes reds. Mellow Orange mutes tattoos and blue-green discolorations. 5 O' Sharp masks beard shadow and can also hide dark circles under the eyes. Each coverup comes in a range of shades to most closely match your actor's skin tone. They're excellent tools to have on hand, particularly for matinee performances after all-night cast parties.

2. Apply an appropriate foundation color over all. Blend into the hairline. Cover the ears, neck, and any skin that will be exposed by the costume.

3. Apply the false eyelashes, using tweezers and eyelash cement. The ends of the individual lashes are dipped in cement, then applied one at a time, as close to

Figure 15.1   Cover any blemishes or beard shadow with the appropriate neutralizing coverup. In this case, we're covering some blemishes with Mellow Yellow.

the natural lash as possible. It's easier if you work from a small amount of cement squeezed onto a plate or a saucer. Position the lashes from about one-third of the way in to the outer corner of the eye, as shown in Figure 15.2 Let the cement dry.

4. Line the eyes with eyeliner.

5. Make up the eyelids. Give them the glamour treatment.

6. Pencil the eyebrows to fill them in and reshape. Bushier eyebrows might need to be tweezed or shaved to give them a more feminine look.

> Depending on the eyebrows of the man you're working on, you may want to block out his existing eyebrows by your favorite method (soap, mortician's wax, spirit gum, or whatever) to give you a clean slate on which to draw in his new, feminine eyebrows.
>
> When using mascara, don't ram the brush into the bottle like you're scrubbing it clean. It adds air to the mascara, which makes it clump and go bad more quickly. Twist the brush from the bottle.

Figure 15.2   Cement the lashes to the outer third of the upper lash, as shown here. Be careful not to cement the actor's eyes shut. Really.

7. Line and color the lips.

8. When the eyelash cement is dry, apply mascara to the lashes.

9. Apply blush to the apples of the cheeks, the chin, and the forehead.

10. Powder to set.

11. Add wig and style.

Naturally, depending on whether the costume will be stepped into or pulled on over the head, you might need to get the actor into costume first, then add the wig and style it. In the latter case, be prepared to touch up the makeup as well or put the makeup on with the actor already in costume.

You can see the final Male-to-Female Drag makeup in Figure 15.3. Oddly enough, our model looks like a newscaster at the television station where he works. Hmm.

To complete this makeup on this model, we would suggest costuming in either a turtleneck or a smart business ensemble with a scarf to hide the model's Adam's apple.

Female-to-Male Drag

Transforming a woman into a man is also a fairly easy task, given the time and the materials. This makeup works with the use of a bald cap and crepe hair beard. Costuming and the use of an elastic bandage to minimize the woman's breasts would complete the illusion.

Again, we're going for a streetwear look. For women, more often than not, believability is not an issue for the makeup; the gag is usually that it's obviously a woman, but no one notices, as in *Servant of Two Masters* and most Shakespearean drag comedies. In these cases, you can get away with a much more simplified and stylized makeup—or even a simple change of costume and a false mustache.

Materials

To complete this makeup as described, you'll need the following supplies:

➲ Hair goo of some sort—styling gel, mousse, something to flatten and control the actor's real hair. Whatever you use should *dry*, so the bald cap won't slip when you apply it

➲ 2 bald caps (you should always have a spare, since they tend to rip or puncture)

➲ Pros-Aide

➲ Adhesive Blending Paste

Figure 15.3   The final Male-to-Female Drag makeup, as worn by our model John Thomas.

➲ Foundation color, crème or liquid

➲ Shadow wheel

➲ Highlight wheel

➲ Greasepaint or rubber mask grease, flesh tones

➲ Cotton swabs

➲ Toothbrush

➲ Spirit gum

➲ Crepe hair, about 1′ each of two colors (we used light brown and auburn)

➲ Gray temporary hair color spray

➲ Wig

We also tried an assortment of hats and eyeglasses on our model.

Preparation

Before you get your actor in the chair, prepare your crepe hair. Since crepe hair comes braided, if you want straight hair, you need to unbraid it, then dip it in hot water and air dry it or blow it dry with a hair dryer. When it's dry, cut it to length; always cut it a little longer than you want, so you can trim and shape the beard after it's applied.

Once it's unbraided and straightened, the crepe hair colors need to be mixed. You should blend two or more colors whenever you're using crepe hair, since natural hair is rarely all one shade.

To blend crepe hair, simply take a length of each color in each hand and begin pulling the hairs apart, a little from each color, and putting them back together in a single bundle. You'll know it's mixed when there is very little striping in the final blend.

When your crepe hair is blended, clip it together with a clothespin, hair clip, or binder clip to keep it from shedding all over the place (it will, anyway, but you can minimize it with a clip).

We also precolored the wig with temporary hair color spray to give it a middle-aged salt-and-pepper look.

The Makeup

To begin, slick your actor's hair back and out of the way. If she has very long hair, you may want to employ a nylon stocking cap to control the excess. Once her hair has been dealt with follow these steps:

1. Fit the bald cap.

2. Lightly mark the position of the actor's ears and any excess latex at the back of the neck. You can also just notch the cap with scissors as an indication of where you want to cut, as shown in Figure 15.4.

3. Remove the bald cap and trim to size, carefully cutting out the ear area.

4. Reapply the bald cap.

5. Working in small sections starting at the center of the forehead, cement the bald cap into place using Pros-Aide applied with a cotton swab or a brush.

6. When you reach the ears, apply the Pros-Aide, then stretch the bald cap into position and hold until the Pros-Aide sets.

7. Do the same for the back of the neck: apply the Pros-Aide, then stretch the bald cap into place and hold it until the adhesive kicks in.

8. Using the Adhesive Blending Paste, fill in the seam of the bald cap along the forehead and down to the ears.

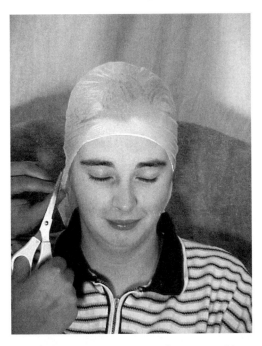

Figure 15.4   Once you have fitted the bald cap on your actor, lightly mark or carefully notch it where you need to cut out ear holes and trim any excess latex.

9. Smooth and blend into the skin with a wet cotton swab or makeup sponge, as shown in Figure 15.5.

The Adhesive Blending Paste can also be used to spackle small tears or punctures in the bald cap. Simply trowel it onto the hole, then blend and smooth into the surrounding latex and let dry or force dry with a hair dryer.

10. Apply flesh-tone greasepaint or rubber mask grease to the forehead area of the bald cap.

11. Apply a matching foundation (the greasepaint or other foundation) to the actor's face, down to just above the chin, where you will be constructing the beard.

12. Add crow's feet around the eyes using your Shadow and Highlight wheels.

13. Accent facial lines—forehead, between the eyebrows, and the creases beside the mouth—with shadow and highlight.

14. Apply spirit gum to the chin and jaw.

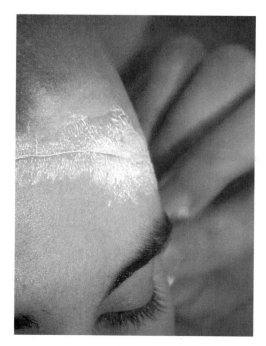

Figure 15.5   Use the Adhesive Blending Paste to fill in and smooth the seam where the bald cap joins the skin.

15. Working in small sections, apply short lengths of your blended crepe hair. Begin below the jawline, and work up toward the lips, then from side to side.

16. Repeat steps 14 and 15, building the beard from the chin, up the planes of the cheeks to the sideburns. You may want to fit the wig at this point to see how high the sideburns need to go. You can see the building process in Figure 15.6.

17. Check for coverage and a natural hairline. Fill in as necessary.

18. Carefully trim and shape the beard with scissors.

19. Gray the beard and eyebrows with temporary hair color spray. It's best to spray it on an old toothbrush and then brush it through the hair.

20. Fit the wig.

21. Adjust makeup as necessary, making sure to blend foundation into the new beard.

22. Powder to set.

23. Dress the makeup with glasses and a hat or whatever masculine headgear and facewear you have handy. You can see the final makeup in Figure 15.7.

Figure 15.6 Working from below the jawline, build the beard in small sections. Work up toward the lips, then side to side.

133

Figure 15.7   The final Female-to-Male Drag makeup, as worn by our model and videographer Colleen McGovern.

Suggested Uses

Well, you just never know when a good drag effect will come in handy. Aside from the obvious roles that require a little cross-dressing (Mary Sunshine in *Chicago*, for one), some nontraditional casting can solve a world of problems.

A recent regional production of Neil Simon's *Lost in Yonkers* had a hell of a time trying to cast the part of the asthmatic Aunt Gert; there were no female actors available for the small but essential role. Rather than scrap the planned production, the company opted to cast a man to play the role in drag. Not only was the drag Gert a success but he had audiences arguing about his gender for weeks after the production. You just never know . . .

16
Satan/Devil/ Demon

Devils, and even *the* devil, make frequent appearances onstage. Mephistopheles, Old Nick, Shaitan, pick a name and run with it. Whether you're involved in a production of a classic like *Faust* or *The Devil and Daniel Webster* or a contemporary morality play for a church or youth group, your devil's got to look his best.

The makeup that follows is a traditional take on the old split foot himself—right down to the horns and goatee. Naturally, images of devils and demons are subject to a wide range of interpretations (all you have to do is check out a few episodes of *The X-Files* and *Buffy the Vampire Slayer* to see what I mean), many of which are full-body makeups that rely heavily on the use of foam latex appliances and bodysuits. Use this makeup as a starting point from which to tailor your own demonic apparition.

Some tailoring will probably be required in any event. The model used here had shaved his head, something that many actors might be unwilling to do. You'll have to alter the design to accommodate the actor's hair, perhaps supplementing it with a traditional widow's peak or other demonizing effect.

Materials

To bring this demon to life, you'll need the following materials:

- Spirit gum
- Crepe hair (black or to match the actor's hair color)
- Pros-Aide or another sturdy adhesive
- Mortician's wax
- Black eyebrow pencil or mascara

⊃ Horns sculpted from Friendly Plastic (as described in Chapter 5)

⊃ Suitably demonic teeth, which also can be made from Friendly Plastic

⊃ Special-effects contact lenses

⊃ Bruise wheel

⊃ Burn wheel

⊃ Red food coloring

⊃ Scissors

⊃ Hair dryer

⊃ Brushes

⊃ Sponges

⊃ Translucent powder

Preparation

It's best to have your crepe hair ready in advance. To prepare it, unbraid it, then dip it in hot water and let it air dry or force it dry with a blow dryer.

When it's dry, cut it into the lengths you want to use. Since we're going with basic black here, no other preparation is necessary.

The Makeup

The first step in creating this makeup is building the crepe hair goatee. As always, whenever using adhesives to attach *anything* to a face, it's a good idea for the actor to shave or depilate the area. This improves adhesion and reduces the potential for pain and irritation during removal.

To begin:

1. Working in small areas, apply a small amount of spirit gum to the chin.

2. Attach 3″ to 6″ lengths of crepe hair, building the goatee from below the chin-line up toward the actor's mouth. You can see the placement of the crepe hair in Figure 16.1.

3. When the chin is covered, repeat the process at the sides of the mouth and above the upper lip, using shorter lengths of crepe hair.

4. You may also want to add a small area of crepe hair under the lower lip for a more groomed look, or fill in the area completely, as we have done here. (A well-groomed demon—go figure.)

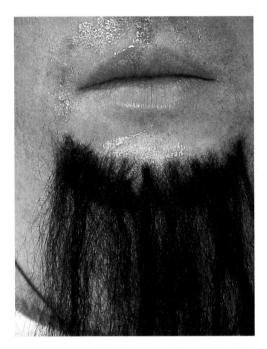

Figure 16.1   Build the goatee from below the chinline up toward the lips, working in small sections as shown.

5. Carefully trim and shape the goatee.

6. Apply a small amount of spirit gum to the outer ends of the eyebrows, following the line of the brow bone.

7. Attach short lengths of crepe hair to the eyebrows, following the direction of the natural brows' growth.

Optionally, you can also fill in between the eyebrows for that unibrow, devil-without-tweezers look.

8. Trim and shape your additions to the eyebrows.

9. Fill in and enhance the natural brows, if necessary, with black eyebrow pencil or mascara.

10. Line the eyes with bruise red from the Bruise wheel.

11. Add—or, as in this case, augment—eye bags in the same bruise red.

12. Shadow lid creases, and contour.

13. Deepen shadows in eye creases with brown from the Shadow wheel.

14. Shadow the sides of the nose and nasolabial creases.

15. Add frown furrows between the eyebrows, crow's feet, and forehead wrinkles.

16. Highlight the shadowed areas.

17. Blend.

18. Shade the hollows of the temples, and draw the shadows back over the skull.

19. Contour the cheeks using the same shadow color.

20. Highlight the temple and cheek shadows and blend.

21. Shadow and highlight the hollows and tendons of the neck, and blend. You can see the shadows in Figure 16.2.

22. Powder to set.

23. Select the spots on the forehead where you will attach the horns, and apply Pros-Aide both to the skin and to the base of the horns.

24. When the Pros-Aide has had a chance to set up (it just takes a minute or two), attach the horns to the head and hold them in place for a moment or two to allow it to bond.

Figure 16.2   Contour the face with shadows and highlights as shown, and blend into the skin.

139

25. While the Pros-Aide dries, color the lips with the same red-brown shade from the Bruise wheel.

26. Apply thin snakes of mortician's wax around the base of the horns and blend them into the skin. This masks the seams and gives the look of natural growth.

27. Make up the mortician's wax with touches of color from the Bruise wheel. You can see a finished horn in Figure 16.3.

28. Touch up the makeup as necessary, checking particularly for smudging around the horns.

29. Powder.

The shine on a shaved or balding head can be a real problem onstage. Powdering it with cornstarch or a combination of cornstarch and talcum powder can reduce and/or eliminate much of the shine.

30. Add the effects contact lenses.

31. Put in the demon teeth.

32. Have the actor swirl a few drops of red food coloring around in his mouth to stain the tongue and teeth bright red.

You can see the final makeup in Figure 16.4.

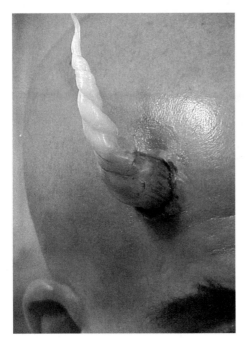

Figure 16.3   Dress the base of the horns with thin circles of mortician's wax and dress the wax with your shadow and highlight colors to blend it into the rest of the makeup.

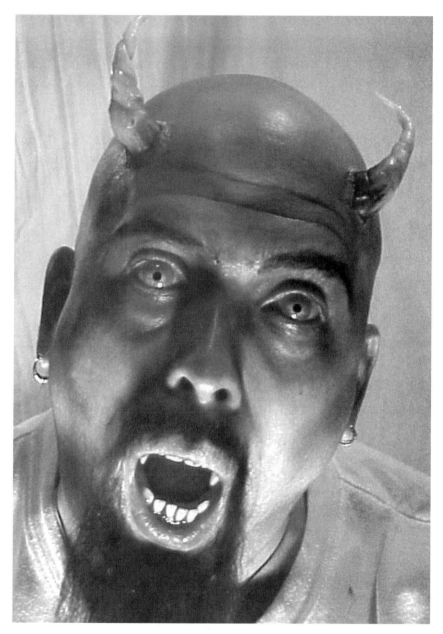

Figure 16.4 The finished demon makeup, as worn by John Pivovarnick, with the addition of a little uplighting for dramatic shadows.

Variations

This makeup is very flexible. While keeping the basic elements of the design intact, simple changes in the color palette and accessory features (such as the beard, horns, contact lenses, and teeth) can completely change both the tenor and the effect of the makeup.

To illustrate that point, compare the final demon makeup shown here with the one presented at the end of Chapter 19, for Shakespeare's Puck. Using essentially the same techniques, with a few additions and subtractions to the design, can create as potentially light and whimsical a character as this one is potentially dark and frightening.

17
Courtly/ Elizabethan

Costume dramas have always been popular and probably always will be. Whether the production at hand is a classical piece (something by Shakespeare, perhaps) or a contemporary piece with a period setting (the Heather Brothers' musical Lust! comes to mind), you may find yourself having to re-create the look of a distant era.

As always, when trying to reproduce an era's look, research is critical.

For the makeup here, we've chosen a courtly and/or Elizabethan look, first, because the look is a staple of classical works, and, second, because the style (with minor variations) works for courtly women over hundreds of years. With further altering, it works for a geisha and can be stylized into Kabuki makeup as well.

In this incarnation, it's an interesting makeup because it involves simulating the look of the high, shaved forehead that was popular with the Elizabethan gentry, without actually shaving the forehead of your actor.

Since we've demonstrated the use of a bald cap in Chapter 15 with the female-to-male drag, we're going to use the soaping method of blocking out a substantial chunk of our model's hair for this makeup. Keep in mind, however, that you can use a bald cap to create the same effect—we just want to put as many tools and techniques as possible at your disposal.

Materials

To execute this makeup, you'll need

- ➲ 1 or 2 bars of soap, preferably white and unscented
- ➲ Water

- ➲ Nylon stocking, cut to fit the area to be soaped
- ➲ Spirit gum
- ➲ Mortician's wax
- ➲ Clown White
- ➲ Baby oil
- ➲ Baby powder
- ➲ Bright lip color
- ➲ Rouge
- ➲ Shadow wheel
- ➲ Eyebrow pencil
- ➲ Period wig
- ➲ Hair dryer, to force the soap dry

Preparation

Soaping out someone's hair requires a little advance preparation because the bar soap needs to be cut up and soaked to soften it up before it can be used.

Depending on how much hair your actor has lengthwise and how much area you need to block out, you may need up to two bars of soap. Better to have too much than not enough, since you can't have your actor wait hours while you soften up some more.

Soap keeps, by the way. You can store any leftover soap in a jar until you need it again. At worst, it will just dry out and you'll need to cut it up and soak it again.

To prepare the soap, cut it up into one-half-inch cubes. You don't have to be anal-retentive about it, but the smaller you cut it up, the faster it softens. Drop it into a shallow dish and fill it with water to cover. Let it soak overnight or about eight to twelve hours. Pour off any remaining water and use the soap left in the bottom of the dish.

You want the soap fairly thick, but thin enough to spread and free of lumps. It will be about the consistency of pudding.

The Makeup

If you were going for a bald effect that was going to be fully seen by the audience, you would carefully part the actor's hair and section it nicely and work in layers from back to front to get a nice, natural-looking hairline. Since, for this makeup, we're simply dressing the model's forehead for a wig, we don't have to be that tidy about it . . . it's sort of a squish, smooth, and move-on process here. Any rough edges at the back of the actor's head will be covered with the wig.

1. Begin saturating the hair with soap at the hairline, and trowel it back with your fingers. Squeegee out the excess with your fingers or a towel. You want to block out the actor's hair to about the crown of the head.

2. Wipe any excess soap from the actor's forehead—it gets everywhere.

3. Force the soap dry with a hair dryer, smoothing the hair as you go. You actually *want* that helmet-head look. You can see what we mean in Figure 17.1.

Figure 17.1   Use the soap to block out the actor's hair from the hairline back to the crown of the head. You want a smooth, if soapy, finish.

4. Apply spirit gum to the actor's forehead about half to three-quarters of an inch from the hairline, starting at the center.

5. Attach the stocking at the center of the forehead and smooth it out. You don't want any wrinkles in the material or a visible seam.

6. Repeat steps 4 and 5 at each side of the forehead; hold the center section in place while you stretch the nylon over the spirit gum toward each ear. You can see the process in Figure 17.2.

7. When the spirit gum is dry, apply another coat of soap to the nylon, stretching the nylon back toward the crown of the head. The soap will hold it in place.

8. Force the soap dry with the hair dryer. You'll end up with a smooth canvas on which to work, like the one shown in Figure 17.3.

9. Block the actor's eyebrows with mortician's wax. You could use soap on them, too, but soap around an actor's eyes makes me nervous.

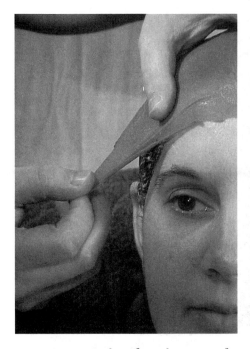

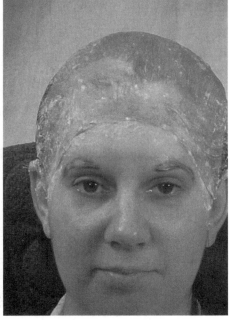

Figure 17.2   Working from the center of the forehead out, attach the nylon stocking with spirit gum, stretching the material to avoid wrinkles.

Figure 17.3   The combination of the soap and nylon give you a smooth, reasonable facsimile of a shaved forehead with which to work.

10. Thin a little Clown White with baby oil to make a white rubber mask grease. It should be thin enough to coat the soaped areas but not thinned to the point where it won't cover. It takes a little experimenting, but the ratio is about three parts Clown White to one part baby oil.

11. Apply the thinned Clown White to the soaped stocking using a makeup sponge.

12. Apply regular Clown White to the actor's face, neck, and ears. You might want to use an angled brush to apply it around the eyes, so you can get it as close as possible. Figure 17.4 shows you how.

13. Depending on the neckline of the actor's costume, you may want to blend the Clown White from the neck to fade into the shoulders and cleavage.

14. Powder to set the Clown White—baby powder works best.

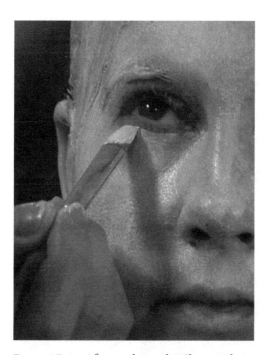

Figure 17.4   After applying the Clown White thinned with baby oil to the soaped stocking, cover the face, neck, and ears with regular Clown White, paying special attention to the eye area. You want to apply the Clown White as close to the eyes as possible.

When working with Clown White, it's easier to powder if you put the baby powder in a baby-sized sock and pat the actor's face with it. The powder seeps through the sock, and the cotton sock doesn't streak the Clown White the way a brush will. When not in use, store the sock in a plastic bag.

That's a tip from an old college friend who went to clown school. Works great.

15. Touch up the Clown White for coverage, if necessary, and powder again.

16. Using the eyebrow pencil, draw in the eyebrows very thin.

17. Heavily rouge the cheeks with a powdered rouge. The fashion was to look like a porcelain doll.

18. Apply lip color to accent the heart shape of the mouth—almost a Clara Bow mouth.

19. Depending on the eyes of the actress and the effect you're going for, you may want to subtly shade the lids and line the eyes with a little eyeliner.

20. Carefully fit the wig to leave a large amount of the forehead exposed, without streaking the Clown White. You can see the fitting of the wig, as well as the rouge, lip, and eye coloring, in Figure 17.5.

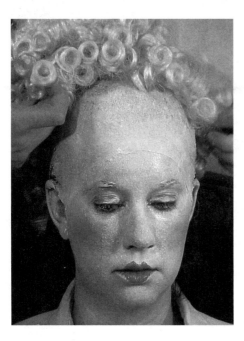

Figure 17.5   After carefully fitting the wig, retouch the makeup as necessary, and repowder to set.

21. Touch up any scuffs in the Clown White, and repowder. You may want to wait until after the actor is in costume, in case there's any damage to the makeup from dressing, too.

You can see the final makeup, in costume, in Figure 17.6. The costume and jewelry complete the effect—and the candlelight doesn't hurt, either.

Figure 17.6   The final makeup, as worn by model Phoebe Sharp, who not only tolerated soap being mashed into her hair but also provided the dress and jewelry.

Suggested Uses

Well, the obvious ones, of course—courtly women in period pieces. Keep in mind the flexibility of the makeup; change the wig and the dress and add a small birthmark (or patch) near the lips, and you have a noblewoman of the French Revolution. The look was popular, with variations in hair and fashion, for well over a century. Foppish men also wore a version of the makeup throughout the same period, but most notably during the French Revolution.

There are contemporary uses for the china doll makeup as well. Modern geishas wear a similar makeup, and the technique can be easily adapted for men playing samurai roles in Kabuki theater.

Part 4
The Supernatural

*U*ntil now, we've been dealing with mainly realistic variations on the human form—granted, we've been abusing the heck out of people, but they've remained *people*.

In this section, we'll deal with creating some of the less real, more esoteric creatures of the stage, from Shakespeare's immortal Puck to legendary creatures such as the wolf man and Frankenstein's creature.

18
The Beast/ Wolf Man

Theater is full of stories of men turned to beasts; *Jekyll and Hyde*, *Beauty and the Beast*, and *A Midsummer Night's Dream* have all been known to turn men into, well, lower forms.

The makeup presented here transforms an average thirty-something man into a hairy, Neanderthal-like beast. It would be appropriate, with minor variations, for a werewolf, Mr. Hyde, an actual Neanderthal, or the Beast of *Beauty and the Beast* fame.

Since this makeup involves a lot of crepe hair, special-effects contact lenses, and mortician's wax, it isn't appropriate for any rapid, onstage transformations unless you've cast two actors, one for before and one for after. For transformations of a lone actor, you're better off relying on wigs, masks, and easily removable facial appliances.

Speaking of crepe hair, this would be a tedious daily process for an extended run. You could relieve much of that tedium by buying or building a wig and beard for the actor (or get him to grow his own) and then supplementing with crepe hair.

Materials

For this makeup you will need

- ➲ About 1 yard each of 2 or 3 colors of crepe hair (we've used two colors here— light and medium brown)
- ➲ Spirit gum
- ➲ Mortician's wax
- ➲ Sculpting tool
- ➲ Vaseline

153

➲ Creme or liquid foundation in a color appropriate to the actor

➲ Shadow wheel

➲ Highlight wheel

➲ Fangs (see Chapter 5 for the how-to on constructing your own)

➲ Effects contact lenses

➲ Blood—optional, but fun

➲ Alcohol or Bond Off! for removal

Preparation

Before you get your actor in the chair, it's best to have your crepe hair prepared. Since crepe hair comes braided, if you want straight hair, you'll need to unbraid it, then dip it in hot water and air dry it or blow it dry with a hair dryer.

When it's dry, you can cut it into the lengths you want to use.

Once it's unbraided and straightened, the crepe hair colors need to be mixed. You should usually blend two or more colors whenever you're using crepe hair, since natural hair is rarely all one shade.

To blend crepe hair, simply take a length of each color in each hand, and begin pulling the hairs apart, a little from each color, and putting them back together in a single clump. You'll know it's mixed when there is very little striping in the final blend.

When your crepe hair is blended, clip it together with a clothespin, hair clip, or binder clip to keep it from shedding all over the place (it will anyway, but you can minimize it with a clip).

For this makeup, we straightened about two-thirds of the crepe hair for use on the model's head and left the other third kinked from the braid to give a different texture to the beard.

We used a *lot* of crepe hair, mainly because the model had recently shaved his head. If you are doing this on an actor with hair (or wearing a suitably beastly wig), match the crepe hair colors to the hair or wig color and use the crepe hair to reshape the hairline and supplement the hair already there.

The Makeup

As always with crepe hair, you're going to work in small areas, applying the spirit gum and then a small amount of hair, following the hair's natural growth pattern. With the head, you work from the hairline back. With beards, work from below the line of the chin up. Applying crepe hair was covered in more detail in Chapter 15, when we did female-to-male drag.

1. Apply spirit gum to scalp, beginning behind the ear.

2. Working in small sections, apply about one-foot lengths of crepe hair from ear to ear to form the hairline. Leave the crepe hair hanging over the actor's face so it doesn't get in the way of subsequent layers.

3. Repeat steps 1 and 2 to lay in a second row of shorter hair, concentrating on the forehead area.

4. Check for coverage and a natural hairline. Fill in as necessary.

5. Repeat, working back from the forehead, until you get the coverage you need—all the way back for a bald head, to the hair- or wigline if you're working with an actor with hair.

6. When the head is complete, flip the hair back into position and out of the actor's face so you can begin to build the beard. Starting below the chinline, apply the spirit gum followed by lengths of the unstraightened crepe hair. You can see the final crepe creation in Figure 18.1.

Figure 18.1 The finished crepe hair application—from bald head to hairball in under an hour.

Handling and sculpting mortician's wax/nose putty is covered in Chapter 5, "3-D Effects."

7. When the beard is complete, begin building up the nose with mortician's wax. Start with a ball of wax applied to the bridge of the nose.

8. Use snakes of wax to block out the actor's eyebrows and begin to build up the brow bone.

9. Add additional mortician's wax to the brow and blend to give that Neanderthal, jutting brow look shown in Figure 18.2.

Depending on the actor's comfort level with wearing contact lenses, you may want to put the contacts in *before* you begin building up the brow. Actors unused to wearing contacts may go through a lot of facial contortions trying to get them in, which can loosen or distort the putty on the nose and brow.

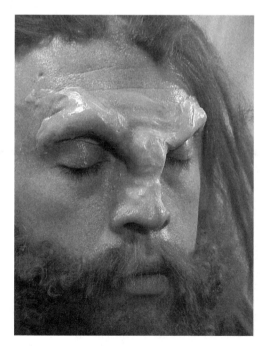

Figure 18.2   Judiciously applied mortician's wax gives the actor the appropriate primitive, jutting brow.

10. Blend the putty into the skin with your fingers or a sculpting tool lightly coated with Vaseline.

11. Sculpt the furrow between the eyes and at the bridge of the nose. When you're done, blot off any excess Vaseline on the putty or skin. You can also press the tissue into the wax for blended texture.

12. Using your Shadow wheel, lay in the shadows around the actor's eyes, and blend the shadows over the putty seams.

13. Lay in the shadows on the rest of the face and in the sculpted furrows of the putty.

14. Sponge on foundation color over all, making sure to work it into the hairlines all around. You can see the applied foundation in Figure 18.3.

15. Adjust the shadows and blend. Pay particular attention to the hairlines and the putty.

16. Use the Shadow wheel to reshape the actor's nostrils, making them larger.

17. Apply your highlights as appropriate to the shadows.

Figure 18.3   The foundation color should be applied evenly over all and worked into the crepe hairlines.

18. Powder to set the makeup; brush off excess.

19. Install the fangs. Dress them up with a little edible stage blood, if you like.

20. Install the contact lenses.

21. Snarl when ready.

You can see the final makeup in Figure 18.4. Depending on the costume, you may need or want to add some additional crepe hair to the actor's chest. Additionally, you may also want to dress the backs and/or palms of the actor's hands—or any other exposed skin—with some hair as well.

Suggested Uses

As mentioned earlier, this makeup is appropriate for a number of beastly stage characters. The basic makeup is very flexible and suitable for a number of uses with changes in the amount and color of hair and a shift in the color palette.

A little less hair and a little more grooming, and he'd be an excellent Mr. Hyde. More hair (starting lower on the forehead and higher on the cheeks) and less grooming will give you an excellent werewolf. Do away with the fangs and dirty him up a bit, and he'd be an interesting take on Caliban in *The Tempest*. He'd also make an excellent troll or ogre for children's theater.

Figure 18.4   The final Beast/Wolf Man makeup, as worn by model John Pivovarnick.

19
Puck

Shakespeare is the source of many immortal characters, both literally and figuratively. People who've never read a single scene of the bard's work recognize Puck's name or the adjective *puckish*, which was coined from it. He created a character whose name became a part of the language. How cool is that?

Puck is a character open to far-ranging interpretations. He's been played by men and boys, women and girls, all of various sizes, shapes, ages, and colors. The most interesting casting I've seen was made by Everett Quinton of the Ridiculous Theatrical Company in New York, when he cast a three hundred-pound woman to play Puck—and she did a remarkable job.

We've gone for a classical interpretation of the sprite here, giving him a glittery look, pointed ears, and a pair of budding horns as a nod to Pan, a character closely related in humor and mischievousness. We've also chosen to put the makeup on a young boy.

Materials

To complete this makeup, you will need

- Foam latex ear tips (available from most makeup supply houses), sized to fit your actor
- Horns (made from Friendly Plastic, as described in Chapter 5)
- Gel body glitter (available in most cosmetic departments that cater to young women)
- Hairstyling gel
- Greasepaint or rubber mask grease, flesh palette
- Liquid foundation, ivory

- ➲ Shadow wheel
- ➲ Eyeliner
- ➲ Powdered eye shadow, neutral
- ➲ Powdered rouge
- ➲ Translucent powder
- ➲ Mortician's wax
- ➲ Vaseline
- ➲ Sculpting tool
- ➲ Pros-Aide or other adhesive
- ➲ Adhesive Blending Paste
- ➲ Makeup sponges
- ➲ Brushes
- ➲ Bond Off! or Detach-All for removal

Preparation

Before you get your actor in the chair, make and style your horns. We sculpted ours out of Friendly Plastic and colored them with alcohol-based design markers, as described in Chapter 5.

You can also save yourself some hassle by making up the ear tips in advance. It's much easier to make them up in your hand than on an actor's head, plus you don't run the risk of knocking them loose in the makeup process. Coat them in greasepaint or rubber mask grease, then shadow the creases. Powder to set the makeup.

The Makeup

To begin, we're going to reshape the model's nose and attach the appliances.

1. Apply a small ball of mortician's wax to the end of the actor's nose.
2. Blend the wax into the skin and shape into an upturned, impish nose, as shown in Figure 19.1.
3. Use a little more mortician's wax to block out about half of the actor's eyebrows so you can reshape the ends. Blend the putty into the skin.
4. Gel the actor's hair, if necessary, so it can be styled around the areas of the forehead where you're going to place the horn buds.

161

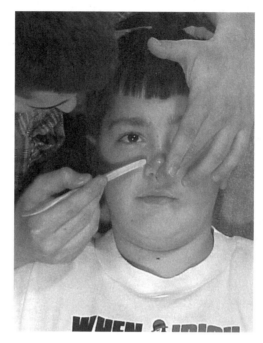

Figure 19.1   The mortician's wax is used to sculpt the model's nose into something upturned and elfin.

5. Mark the position where the horns are going; check for evenness and symmetry.

6. Apply Pros-Aide to the skin where the horns will be applied.

7. Coat the ends of the horns with Pros-Aide as well, for a better bond.

8. Let the Pros-Aide dry a little, then apply the horns, as shown in Figure 19.2.

Pros-Aide is a heavy-duty adhesive made by ADM Tronics. You get an incredible bond with it, it's water-soluble until it dries, and it requires an equally heavy-duty substance to remove it. You'll need Bond Off! or Detach-All.

See the resource appendix at the end of the book for contact information for ADM Tronics. If you don't have or don't want to get Pros-Aide, you can use another adhesive for both the horns and the ears, such as liquid latex or spirit gum, but the bond won't be as secure.

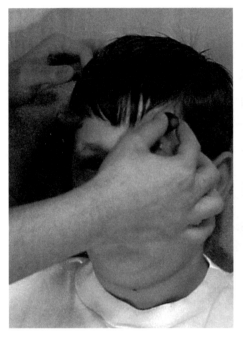

Figure 19.2 Attach the horns, making sure they're placed evenly and symmetrically. You don't want to have to remove and replace them.

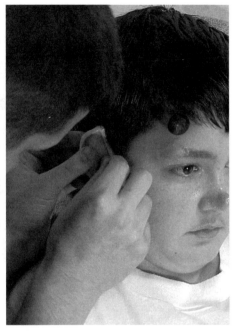

Figure 19.3 Mask any gaps or seams around the ear appliances with adhesive Blending Paste before applying foundation.

9. Apply the ear tips, also with Pros-Aide, following the same steps as for applying the horn buds.

10. Let the Pros-Aide dry.

11. Fill in any gaps between the ear and the ear tips with Adhesive Blending Paste, as shown in Figure 19.3. Trowel it on with your finger, then smooth with a wet makeup sponge.

> Adhesive Blending Paste is the makeup equivalent of spackle for plasterboard. A very handy product, it allows you to fill in any gaps, seams, and even small holes and tears in a foam latex appliance. It's a product of Michael Davy Film & TV Makeup. It's proven a valuable tool for us. See the resource appendix at the end of the book for contact information.

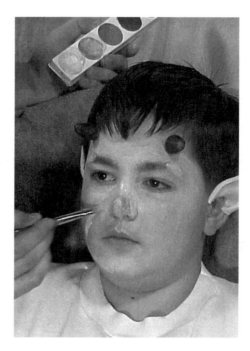

Figure 19.4   Apply foundation color and
blend into the appliances for a seamless
look.

12. Apply foundation color over all. You've already used a greasepaint or rubber
    mask grease to make up the ears in advance. Use the same makeup on the
    face, neck, and ears, or choose a matching color in a liquid or crème makeup.
    We used a combination of white and a light flesh-tone greasepaint for a lu-
    minous look and to show off the glitter. You can see the foundation colors
    going on in Figure 19.4.

13. Using your Shadow wheel, fill in and reshape the ends of the masked eye-
    brows. Draw the ends up a little, if you like.

14. Line the eyes with eyeliner.

15. Shade the eyelids in neutral beiges and browns.

16. Apply glitter gel over all.

> Don't forget, depending on Puck's costume, you'll want to make up any
> and all exposed skin, at the very least with the glitter gel.

17. Use a neutral/natural lip color to color and define the lips.

18. Blush the apples of the cheeks, the forehead, the nose, and the chin using a powdered, ruddy blush.

You've got yourself a sprite who's ready to wreak havoc. You can see the final makeup in Figure 19.5.

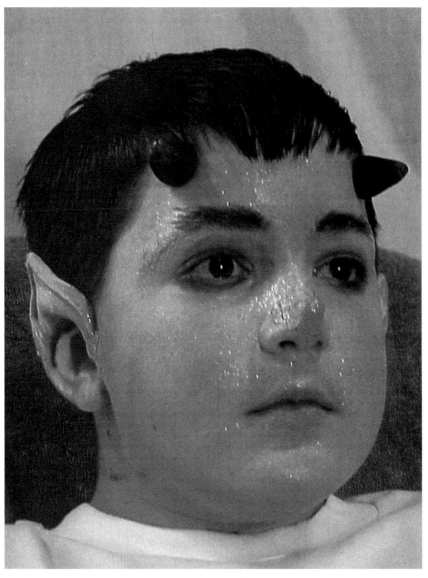

Figure 19.5   The finished Puck makeup, as worn by model James McGurl.

Suggested Uses

This is a flexible design that can be adapted for many uses. With the addition of a crepe hair goatee, chest hair, and the right costume, this design works for a faun like Mr. Tumnus in *The Lion, The Witch, and the Wardrobe*. Change the color palette to a redder range, and you have an imp, devil, or demon. Use any nonstandard foundation color (gray, blue, green—anything), and you have an interesting alien life-form.

Keep in mind as you're putting your design together that Friendly Plastic is very simple to sculpt and reshape. You can take the horns, and other add-on appendages, as far as your imagination and your adhesive will allow.

20
The Bird

Humanity's interest in birds stems much from jealousy, I think—we have to work so hard to fly. Birds' natural grace, ability to soar at will, and endless array of colors have made them a natural metaphor for all the things we, as people, are not.

As such, birds make frequent appearances as characters onstage, in plays as wide-ranging as children's theater productions of *Alice in Wonderland* and productions of Aristophanes' *The Birds*.

Depending on the production, you may want to resort to bird masks rather than makeup to facilitate character changes for an ensemble cast, as with the Manhattan Project's adaptation of *Alice in Wonderland*, where a cast of five plays all the characters from the book. Other productions may need to rely on simple paint effects with the addition of a prosthetic beak.

For our purposes, we've opted for a fairly simple yet effective dimensional makeup that looks very realistic—well, considering that it's on a person. It combines a partial mask with a liberal application of feathers. In an actual production, it would also rely heavily on the costume to complete the illusion.

Materials

For this makeup, you will need

- ➲ Hard-plastic bird mask with a good beak (we picked one up at a local costume shop for about four dollars)
- ➲ Black gloss enamel spray paint
- ➲ Scissors
- ➲ Implement of fire (lighter, match candle)
- ➲ Hot-melt glue gun and glue sticks (don't worry, none of this goes on the actor)   **167**

⊃ About 8 ounces of white feathers (available in craft stores)

⊃ Nylon stocking (optional)

⊃ Spirit gum

⊃ Black greasepaint or crème

⊃ Clown White

⊃ Yellow contact lenses (optional)

The Mask

We started with a plastic, full-face puffin mask (the kind kids wear at Halloween) that we found at a local costume shop. It was mostly white with a red, black, and orange beak. The shape of the beak was interesting, but the colors were kind of garish, so we spray painted it a gloss black and let it dry.

When the mask was dry, we fitted it on the model and measured where we wanted to cut. We cut the mask so that only the forehead and top half of the beak remained, as well as the elastic to hold it on the model's face. We left a generous area around the eyes to keep from obstructing the model's vision.

The trimmed mask edges were very sharp, so we melted the edges a little with a lighter to smooth out any rough spots and protect our model's face.

Then we trimmed and applied the white feathers in overlapping layers, much like fish scales or roofing shingles, using the hot-melt glue gun. The feathers were glued from the top of the mask down and overlapped to hide the quill end. You can see the arrangement of feathers on the finished mask in Figure 20.1.

Once the mask has been feathered, you're ready to feather the actor. Before you begin, however, prepare the feathers by cutting away any excess quill and fluff.

> When using a hot-melt glue gun, be careful not to burn yourself or melt a hole in the plastic mask. Of course, if you do make a hole in the mask, you can always hide it with feathers.

The Makeup

The makeup is very much a repeat of the process for feathering the mask; just substitute spirit gum for the hot-melt glue.

1. Beginning near the ear, lay in a coat of spirit gum about an inch square. You want to work in small areas.

Figure 20.1   The finished bird mask, ready for the actor.

Figure 20.2   Apply the feathers, beginning about an inch below the eye, and work down the cheek toward the chin.

2. Apply the trimmed feathers quill end toward the eye, leaving about an inch or so of exposed skin below the eye.

3. Work down the cheek toward the chin. You can see the arrangement of feathers in Figure 20.2.

4. Repeat the process on the other side of the face.

5. Put the mask on the actor (as shown in Figure 20.3) to make sure the mask and facial feathers meet.

6. Fill in with additional feathers as necessary.

7. Make up the actor's ears and neck with Clown White.

8. Make up the exposed skin around the actor's eyes with black greasepaint or crème.

9. Powder to set the makeup.

10. Put the yellow contact lenses in the actor's eyes.

11. Fit the mask to the actor's face.

Figure 20.3   With the mask in place, check the makeup for adequate feather coverage, especially where the mask meets the actor's skin.

Depending on the actor's comfort level with wearing contact lenses, you may want to put them in *before* applying makeup around the eyes. Our model had never worn contacts before, and the makeup around the eyes was smeared several times, first with the attempt to place the contacts, then with the natural tearing common with first-time contact wearing. As always, you should be very careful with contact lenses—both putting them in and applying makeup around them—as misuse can injure the actor's eyes.

You can see the finished makeup in Figure 20.4. For a rather simple makeup, the final effect is rather startling.

Depending on the costume, you may want to use a nylon stocking to cover the crown of the actor's head, then spirit gum additional feathers to the stocking. You could also use white hair spray to whiten the actor's hair to blend with the feathers.

Figure 20.4   The finished bird, as modeled by Mike McGurl.

Suggested Uses

This makeup is appropriate for any play calling for a speaking bird character, such as the Dodo and other birds in *Alice in Wonderland*, when a quick character change is not required. The feathers *do* take some plucking afterward, not to mention a healthy dose of alcohol, spirit gum remover, or Bond Off! to get rid of the spirit gum.

This makeup can be easily modified into any sort of bird, as long as you can find or build an appropriate beak and track down the right color feathers.

21
The Thing

This makeup is sort of a generic fantasy creature—part Wicked Witch of the West, part boogeyman, part troll. It's more about expanding on the gelatin technique to get a more refined, sculpted effect than you've previously seen in Chapter 10, "The Disfigured," and Chapter 13, "Leprosy."

The makeup that follows creates a stylized creature that can be adapted to fit many of your evil-being needs. With modification, the Thing would be useful for any number of productions requiring a somewhat grotesque creature or creatures—and also a lot of fun for haunted houses and the like.

As with the other gelatin techniques, it is only appropriate for short-term use and not at all appropriate for a strenuous or quick-change role. For a longer-lasting makeup, you might want to consider casting appliances out of foam or slush latex.

> You can increase the durability of a gelatin makeup by substituting glycerin for about half of the water you would normally use.

This makeup also uses special-effects contact lenses, which can slightly impair the actor's vision, and homemade prosthetic teeth (covered in Chapter 5), which can affect pronunciation and diction. For a speaking role, you'll either want to eliminate the teeth or go with commercial dental appliances that will have less of an impact on the actor's speech.

Materials

To execute this makeup, you will need the following supplies:

➲ Unflavored gelatin (Knox is preferred)

➲ Toilet paper

- ➲ Liquid foundation in an appropriate shade
- ➲ MagiCake aqua palettes, Clown and Fantasy
- ➲ Green food coloring
- ➲ Translucent powder
- ➲ Hair dryer
- ➲ 1″ or 2″ paint brush
- ➲ Makeup brushes
- ➲ Makeup sponges
- ➲ Towels
- ➲ Effects contact lenses (optional)
- ➲ Prosthetic teeth

Preparation

This makeup uses the same gelatin concoction used in Chapters 10 and 13. Before you get your actor in the chair, it's best to have the gelatin cooked and cooled to the point where it can be safely applied to the actor's face.

You'll need two batches: one made from about eight to ten packets of gelatin and approximately one and a half cups of water and a smaller batch made with four packs of gelatin and about one-half cup of water, which you will tint with green MagiCake aqua cake and food coloring. The smaller batch won't be needed until later in the makeup, but you can prepare it in advance and reheat it just before you need it.

You'll also find it saves some time and aggravation if you prepare about twenty-five to thirty lengths of toilet tissue (three to five squares each) beforehand. While working with the gelatin, your fingers tend to get very sticky, and wrestling with tissue becomes something like an old vaudeville routine.

As mentioned in Chapter 13, nuking a moist cloth towel in a microwave oven gives you a steaming towel that almost instantly dissolves accumulated gelatin from your fingers. If you don't have access to a microwave, wash your hands frequently in warm, soapy water. You can also give your hands a quick, light coat of Vaseline before you start, to prevent sticking.

The Makeup

With the prep work out of the way, you're ready to begin.

> To add volume to the makeup without adding additional weight, your lengths of tissue should be twisted or wadded into an approximation of the shape you want, then applied dry to the face. Coat the tissue with gelatin. Next, apply a layer of flat tissue over the wadded/twisted tissue to give a smoother surface, then paint the flat tissue with gelatin.
>
> This procedure holds true for all the tissue application in this makeup, unless otherwise noted in the step-by-step instructions.

1. Coat the actor's head—face and hair—with a layer of gelatin. Test the temperature first.

2. Air or force dry with a hair dryer until the gelatin is tacky to the touch.

3. Begin building up around the eye sockets with short lengths of toilet tissue. Follow the bone structure of the eye socket.

4. Coat the applied tissue with gelatin. You can see the application process begin in Figure 21.1.

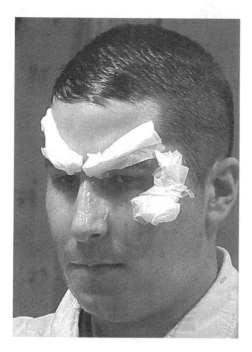

Figure 21.1 First, begin building up around the eye sockets with tissue to create that deep-set eye look.

5. Repeat steps 3 and 4 to continue building up the rest of the actor's face, as shown in Figure 21.2. You're free to work in any order you care to, but these are the areas we built up, in the order we did them:

- ⊃ Eye sockets
- ⊃ Forehead
- ⊃ Cheeks
- ⊃ Chin
- ⊃ Further up forehead, continuing over hairline
- ⊃ Over nose and down cheeks

6. Once the face has been sculpted into shape (you can see the rough shaping of the face in Figure 21.3), brush a coating of gelatin over all.

7. If necessary, force dry until the gelatin is tacky; then you can begin adding detail to the rough shape.

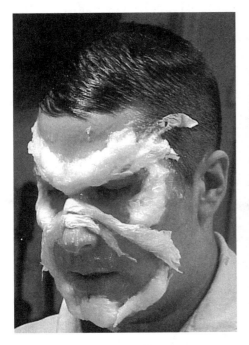 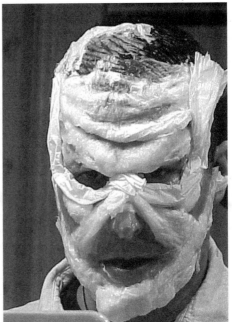

Figure 21.2   Continue adding tissue to build up the actor's face, following the natural lines and bone structure of the face but exaggerating them to grotesque proportions. Neatness doesn't particularly count at this stage.

Figure 21.3   Use the tissue technique to build up the actor's face as shown here, then apply a coating of gelatin over all.

8. In detailing, you'll add additional prominences to the rough shape with twisted lengths of tissue. These are the areas we detailed, in the order we did them:

   ⊃ From the sides of the nose up to the temples

   ⊃ Tip of the nose

   ⊃ Forehead, adding furrows

   ⊃ Planes of the cheeks, beside the ears

   ⊃ Big eye bags beneath the eyes

   ⊃ V-furrow between the brows

   ⊃ Upper lip

9. Once the face has been detailed (you can see the detail work in Figure 21.4), apply a layer of flat tissue over all, and brush with a coating of gelatin.

10. Force dry with a hair dryer.

11. Apply translucent powder over all to absorb any residual moisture.

Figure 21.4. Additional tissue applications add detail to the rough shape shown in Figure 21.3. A dark green MagiCake aqua is then applied to the creases and shadow areas to act almost like an underpainting.

12. Using the MagiCake aqua palette, mix deep green with a little black to get a very dark green. Paint the eye sockets with the dark green.

13. Using the same dark green, paint the creases of the face and other shadow areas with a small brush.

14. Apply a coating of the thick green gelatin over all. Be sure to get good coverage of the white tissue underneath.

With thick enough gelatin (and it will thicken up on you), you can get some interesting drip/melting effects by letting the gelatin run over portions of the actor's face. If you have any gelatin left over, try it and see what you can do with it. Flesh-colored gelatin is excellent for creating the appearance of melting skin.

15. Force dry the green gelatin.

16. If necessary, touch up the color coverage with the MagiCake aqua green. Make sure to color all exposed skin as well.

17. We left the gelatin as is to give the creature a slimy look. If you care to, you can powder the whole makeup using the dry green MagiCake cake as a pressed powder; it just won't look slimy.

18. Add the prosthetic teeth.

19. Put in the effects contact lenses.

You can see the final Thing in Figure 21.5.

Suggested Uses

As mentioned at the beginning of the chapter, this is not an appropriate makeup to use for a physically strenuous role, but it's ideal for relatively brief stage appearances, film work (where you have a lot of time available for retouching), and haunted houses and other interactive entertainment where the element of surprise is a key factor.

This makeup can be easily adapted to multiple effects simply by changing the color palette and the application of the tissue. Go to the red range of color and minimize the tissue to create a very effective full-head acid/radiation burn. Flesh tones will give you the effect of melting skin.

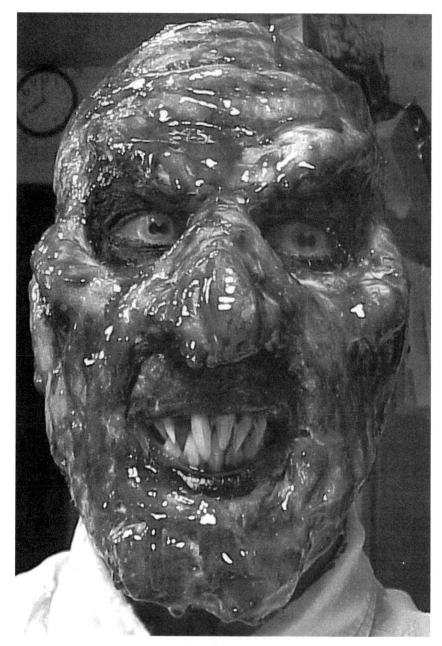

Figure 21.5   The final Thing makeup, as worn by our model David Sartor.

22
The Creature

*E*ver since Mary Shelley's creation *Frankenstein* shocked Victorian England, the world has been fascinated by Victor Frankenstein's monster. Assembled from cadavers and bits and pieces stolen from hospitals, the creature has been subject to dozens of interpretations as wildly different as Karloff's creature in the original Universal feature film, to the blond boy-toy version in *Rocky Horror Picture Show*, to Peter Boyle's take on him in *Young Frankenstein*.

The monster (or just monster wanna-bes) makes numerous appearances both onstage and in film. The challenge to the designer is to come up with an interpretation that meets the demands of the play and fulfills the audience's expectations, yet doesn't infringe on Universal's copyright of the original flat-topped, bolt-necked, leather-upholstered version of the monster. Frankenstein may be scary, but copyright and entertainment lawyers are scarier still.

Additional considerations include

- Makeup permanence versus the amount of stage time the creature has
- The effect that elaborate dimensional makeup around the actor's mouth and eyes might have on his ability to speak and see
- The impact that the cost of doing foam latex prosthetics will have on the production

For the sake of a moderately priced makeup with reasonable permanence and no interference with the actor's ability to speak, we've chosen a creature effect that relies on applied mortician's wax (which sounds way cooler than nose putty for this particular makeup) and paint rather than elaborate latex appliances. We've opted for *one* special contact lens to minimize danger to the actor and because mismatched eyes reinforce the assembled feeling of the creature. Your budget may or may not allow for contacts at all.

The model here wears his hair—well, what little hair he has—in a very short buzz cut, which simplifies the process of making up his full head. If your actor is unwilling to buzz or shave his head, you may have to resort to a bald cap (covered in Chapter 15) or rework the design to accommodate the actor's hair.

Materials

For this makeup, you will need

- Bruise kit
- Two foundation colors: one a few shades lighter than the actor's skin, the second to match the actor's skin
- Contour wheel of shadow and highlight colors
- Eyebrow pencil
- Black or brown eyeliner (pencil or liquid)
- Liquid latex
- Mortician's wax
- Vaseline
- Translucent powder
- Black leather twine cut into 25–30 ¼"–½" lengths
- Red, green, and yellow food coloring or temporary tooth stain
- Gel blood
- Makeup sponges and brushes
- Opaque/cataract contact lens

Additionally, you might want to have a hair dryer to force dry the latex.

The Makeup

To begin, as always, the actor's face should be clean of all dirt, makeup, and skin oils so the makeup has the best adhesion possible.

1. Faintly sketch in scar positions with eyebrow pencil, as shown in Figure 22.1. We're using a pattern that goes from upper left to lower right, circling the eye, with a secondary Y-shaped scar on the upper right of the forehead. We're also using putty to block out the model's left eyebrow.

181

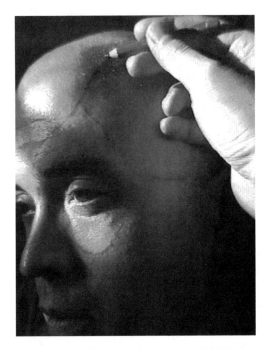

Figure 22.1   Sketch the scar pattern lightly on the actor's skin as a guide for laying down the mortician's wax.

2. Paint the scar areas with liquid latex, about one inch wide. Allow to dry or force dry with a hair dryer. You *don't* want to apply the latex to the actor's eyebrow; he would be picking it out for days afterward.

3. Coat your hands *lightly* with Vaseline to prevent the mortician's wax from sticking to them, then roll mortician's wax into snakes.

Caution: If you use too much Vaseline, the putty will lose its stickiness. If that happens, wash and dry your hands and work the putty until it gets sticky again.

4. Position the wax snakes over the dried latex and press into position.

5. Lightly grease fingertips, if necessary, and blend the edges of the wax snakes into the skin (see Figure 22.2 for details).

6. Sculpt seams into the mortician's wax using a butter knife or a sculpting tool. Again, a little Vaseline will keep the wax from sticking to your fingers or the

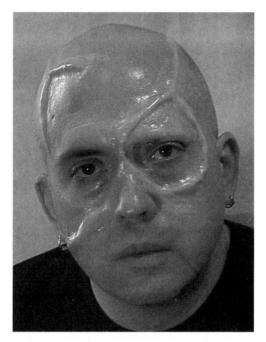

Figure 22.2   Use your lightly greased
fingertips to blend the mortician's wax into
the actor's skin.

sculpting tool. When you're finished sculpting, blot any excess Vaseline from
the scars.

7. Seal the mortician's wax with latex and let dry.

> Caution: It's not a good idea to force dry the latex you use to seal the
> mortician's wax because the wax may soften and melt. If your hair dryer
> has a cool setting, that should work.

8. Using the foundation color that matches the actor's skin, apply foundation to
   the top of the head to the main scar line and around the scarred eye.

9. Apply the foundation that's about two shades lighter than the actor's skin to
   the rest of the face, neck, and other exposed skin, including the scars.

10. Shade the actor's bone structure—temples, cheeks, chin, eye sockets—using
    a darker, almost brown, flesh tone. Figure 22.3 shows you how. Note that the
    makeup is heavier than necessary to compensate for the lightening effect of
    powdering.

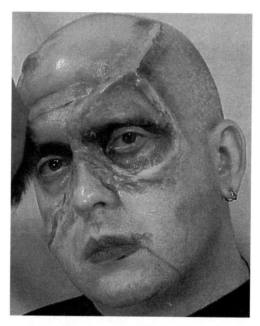

Figure 22.3   Deep shadows, accented with bruise colors, pop the dimensionality of the scar material.

11. Use your bruise kit to add random bruises to the actor's face and neck, particularly around the scars. If necessary, touch up the highlights on the raised scar areas.

12. Mottle the lips bluish-purple from the bruise kit.

13. Paint on varicose veins using brown, red, and purple. Figure 22.4 shows you the placement of paint for our design. For the scar near the mouth, you can use paint or a rigid collodion, as discussed in Chapter 5.

14. Use translucent powder to set the makeup.

15. Dress the seam of the sculpted scars with gel blood for that "just stitched" look.

16. Apply the stitches by pressing the pieces of leather twine into the mortician's wax. Place lengthwise across the wax, avoiding too regular or tidy of an arrangement. Stitches were a new medical technology in the Victorian era; besides, it looks nastier when the stitches are rough and irregular.

If the wax doesn't want to hold the stitches, a dab of latex or spirit gum will help. Use tweezers to dip the stitches in your adhesive and press them into place on the mortician's wax.

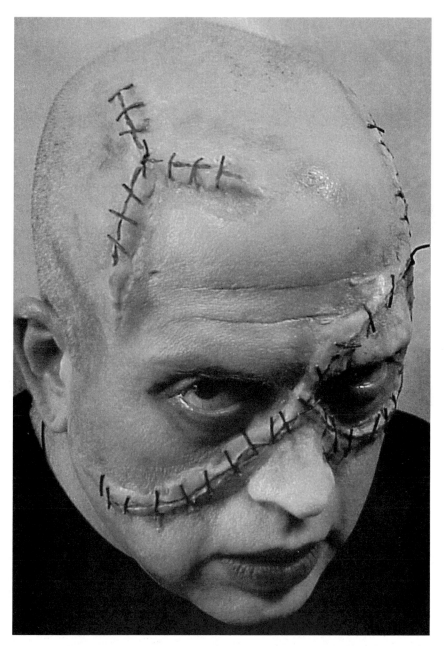

Figure 22.4   The finished makeup under indoor lighting, with attitude. Actors! (Model: John Pivovarnick)

17. Mix equal parts of red, green, and yellow food coloring (just a few drops each) and have the actor swish the food coloring mix around his mouth to temporarily discolor his teeth. This may need to be reapplied throughout the performance. If necessary, keep a small cup of the food coloring mix on the prop table or somewhere the actor has easy access to. You can also use pre-pared tooth colorings, like Ben Nye's Tooth Color line; a combination of Nicotine and Zombie Rot work well together.

18. Put in the cataract contact lens.

You can see the finished makeup in Figure 22.5, shot in natural, unfiltered sunlight, the harshest test any makeup can pass. Just to see the effect lighting can have on makeup, note the difference in appearance between Figure 22.5, natural sunlight (and imagine the surprise of passersby as the photo was taken), and Figure 22.4, which was taken indoors under tungsten lighting without a flash.

Suggested Uses

Well, *Frankenstein*, of course, and any of the Frankenstein variations. However, don't underestimate the flexibility of the technique. With a more subtle treatment (using rigid collodion instead of mortician's wax and finer material and placement for the stitches), this technique will work for

- ➲ Recent surgery patients
- ➲ Accident victims
- ➲ Post-autopsy cadavers
- ➲ Zombies

And it's a real kick in the pants around Halloween.

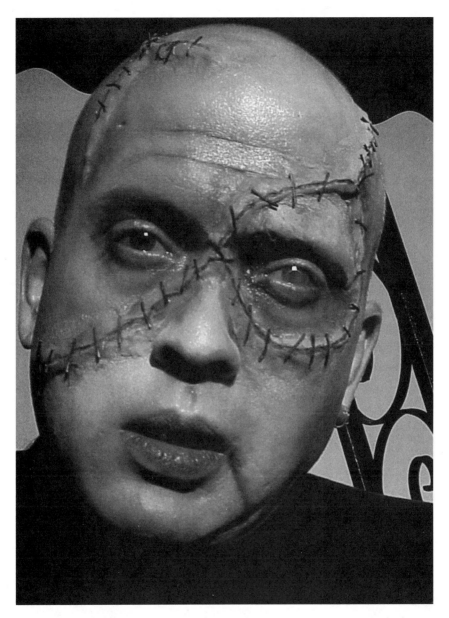

Figure 22.5   The final makeup in direct sunlight.

Appendix A: Cleaning Up Your Act

It's a rude, evil effects makeup artist who doesn't show his actors the proper way to remove the makeup that's been applied or provide them with any special solvents needed to painlessly remove an elaborate makeup.

In addition to being evil, it's also counterproductive. When an actor rips and runs without properly removing a makeup, any damage done to the skin—abrasions, rashes, and/or acne—might complicate the reapplication of the makeup, so it's in your own best interests to show an actor the ropes.

Removal and Cleanup

There are several methods of removal and cleanup that range from basic cold cream followed by soap and water to chemical solvents used to dissolve sturdy adhesives.

Basic Paint Effects

Basic paint effects can easily be removed by traditional means: slather on a healthy amount of cold cream, wipe it off with facial tissue, and wash with soap and water.

Most theatrical makeup companies also sell prepared liquid makeup removers, specifically designed to cut through greasepaint and heavy theatrical makeup. These should also be followed up with soap and water and a moisturizer.

Collodion

Collodion used for scars and other effects can usually be peeled from the skin. If the collodion has a good grip, however, or is applied over hair, you can buff the collodion off with a washcloth that's been dipped in isopropyl alcohol. It doesn't *remove* the collodion, but it makes it brittle and easier to remove by peeling. You can also resort to a stronger solvent like Bond Off! or Detach-All.

Collodion and the solvents used to remove it can have a very drying effect on the skin. Make sure your actors wash well with soap and water after removal, then follow up with a moisturizer.

Gel Effects

Effects gels (whether cooked up by you or manufactured), like Flesh Effects or Scar Effects Gel, are easily removed. Simply peel the gel gently from the skin. Any residue can be removed by washing with warm, soapy water or with the assistance of a little alcohol on a washcloth.

Appliances

Depending on the adhesives used to apply them, most appliances can be gently peeled from the skin, and the adhesives can then be removed using one of the solvents listed in the following section.

If the appliance won't peel off easily, you can wet the edges with a solvent-soaked cotton swab until the adhesive loosens. Peel a little, then soak a little, repeating until the appliance comes off.

Adhesives

Different adhesives take different solvents for removal.

➲ Latex can usually be peeled from the skin or rubbed into little latex pellets and washed off. A little alcohol on a soft cloth will help remove any latex remaining on the skin.

➲ Spirit gum is notoriously difficult to remove, since it never really dries. Alcohol can take it off; gently scrub the area with a washcloth soaked in alcohol. There are also prepared solvents made to remove spirit gum and its sticky residue; most are called spirit gum remover, oddly enough.

➲ Medical adhesives are designed not to come unstuck easily. You will need to use a sturdy solvent like Bond Off! or Detach-All to remove them.

➲ Pros-Aide, like medical adhesives, doesn't let go willingly. You can buff it off with baby oil on a washcloth, or you can use the official Pros-Aide Remover from ADM Tronics. Bond Off! and Detach-All will also undo Pros-Aide's hold on your skin.

A Word About Solvents

Solvents make removing effects makeup a simple affair; however, many of them are very harsh to sensitive skin.

Isopropyl alcohol can have a drying effect. As for prepared solvents, I've seen actors with very sensitive skin break out in burnlike rashes after using some of these products. You might want to do a patch test on your actors' inner arms before you use any such harsh chemicals on their faces, particularly if they warn you of sensitive skin.

Whenever you resort to using a solvent to remove makeup or an appliance, you should make sure that your actors wash well with soap and water to remove any residue, and you should advise them to follow up with a moisturizer.

Skin Care After the Fact

Actors who go through a daily routine of skin abuse from makeup, and especially effects makeup, must counter with a daily routine of moisturizing and healing, or else they could suffer from skin irritation, dryness, acne, or rashes.

You should warn your actors about the potential reactions to the makeup. Recommend skin care products and moisturizers to help avoid and repair skin damage. Occasional exfoliation with a good facial scrub will help remove any dry, dead skin cells. Have them follow up with a moisturizer, preferably one with vitamin E and/or aloe.

> Moisturizers should be applied *after* makeup removal, not before application. Moisturizers under an effects makeup will shorten the life of the makeup.

Naturally, if any actor has a serious allergic reaction to a makeup, the makeup should be redesigned to eliminate the problem element, whether it's an adhesive, a latex appliance, or a particular brand of makeup.

Helping an actor keep his or her skin in good condition will also make your job easier; there will be less whining as you try to coax him or her into the chair night after night.

Appendix B:
Suppliers and Distributors

The list of suppliers and manufacturers that follows should help you build up your own arsenal of effects supplies.

Those that we've dealt with and can recommend are indicated with a dagger symbol (†); that's not to say that the others aren't dandy as well, just that we have no personal experience with them. You'll have to try them out for yourself.

Keep in mind that the Internet and search engines such as Yahoo! (*www.yahoo.com*) and Lycos (*www.lycos.com*), among others, are excellent sources of up-to-the-minute information about FX makeup supplies, new products, and distributors. A simple search on Yahoo!, using *special effects makeup* as the search phrase, netted more than *eleven thousand* returns. That's a lot of information, not all of it relevant, but a great starting place.

Our List

ADM Tronics, Inc.†, Makers of Pros-Aide and other prosthetic essentials
224-S Pegasus Avenue, Northvale, New Jersey 07647
Phone: (201) 767-6040
Fax: (201) 784-0620
E-mail: *pegasuslabs@juno.com* or *sales@admtronics.com*
Web: *admtronics.com*

Alcone Co.†, makeup, stage blood, rigging equipment, theatrical supply house
5-49 49th Avenue, Long Island City, New York 11101
Phone: (718) 361-8373

American Art Clay Co. (AMACO), manufacturers of Friendly Plastic
Phone: (800) 374-1600
Fax: (317) 248-9300
E-mail catalog requests to: *catalog@amaco.com*
192   Web: *www.amaco.com*

Ben Nye[†], manufacturer of all manner of makeup and effects products
5935 Bowcroft Street, Los Angeles, California 90016
Phone: (310) 839-1984
Fax: (310) 839-2640

Burman Industries, Inc.[†], special-effects makeup, mold- and model-making
supplies; extensive catalog, our source for Friendly Plastic, premade appliances,
and bald caps
14141 Covello Street, Suite 10-C, Van Nuys, California 91405
Phone: (818) 782-9833
Fax: (818) 782-2863
E-mail: info@burmanfoam.com
Web: www.burmanfoam.com

Graftobian, manufactures a line of theatrical makeup supplies; no direct sales;
distributor information on website
510 Tasman Street, Madison, Wisconsin 53714
Phone: (608) 222-7849
Fax: (608) 222-7893
E-mail: makeup@graftobian.com
Web: www.graftobian.com

Kryolan Corp.[†], manufacturer of makeup and effects supplies, including rigid
collodion; no direct sales; distributor information on website
132 Ninth Street, San Francisco, California 94103-2603
Phone: (415) 863-9684
Fax: (415) 863-9059
Web: www.kryolan.com

LensQuest[†], special-effects contact lenses, as well as regular prescription lenses
128 Cherry Street, Marietta, Georgia 30060
Phone: (770) 429-3901
Fax: (770) 424-4341
Web: www.lensquest.com

Mainstage Theatrical Supply, Theatrical, television, and film supplies of every
variety, including makeup
129 W. Pittsburgh Avenue, or 2515 W. Cervantes Street, Milwaukee, Wisconsin
53204
Phone: (414) 278-0878 or (800) 236-0878
Fax: (414) 278-0986
Web: www.mainstage.com

Mehron, Inc., theatrical makeup and supplies
Phone: (800) 332-9955
E-mail: *info@mehron.com*
Web: *www.mehron.com*

Michael Davy Film and TV Makeup[†], makers of Collodacolor colored collodion, Sweat Stop, and Adhesive Blending Paste
Michael Davy Film & TV Makeup, PO Box 570309, Orlando, Florida 32857
Phone:(888) 225-7026
E-mail: *michael.davy@mci2000.com*
Web: *www.bitstorm.net/mdftv*

The Monster Makers, online catalog of FX supplies, specializing in sculpting, mold making, and foam latex supplies
7305 Detroit Avenue, Cleveland, Ohio 44102
Phone: (216) 651-7739
Fax: (216) 631-4329
E-mail: *sales@monstermakers.com*
Web: *www.monstermakers.com*

Norcostco, Inc.[†], theatrical supplies, including makeup and effects; locations nationwide; visit website to find a location near you
Web: *www.norcostco.com/norcost.htm*

Special Effect Supply Co., provides hard-to-find information and materials to special-effects artists and other craftspersons throughout the world
164 East Center Street #A, North Salt Lake, Utah 84054
Phone: (801) 936-9762 or (orders) (888) 648-8810
Fax: (801) 936-9763
Web: *www.fxsupply.com*

Stage Supply dot Com[†], online sales of makeup and theatrical supplies, including the full line of Ben Nye products
803 Highland Drive, Chambersburg, Pennsylvania 17201
E-mail: *sales@stagesupply.com*
Web: *www.stagesupply.com*

Your List

Don't overlook the resources in your own backyard. Most communities have at least one or more resources for theatrical supplies in the vicinity. Check your phone book for local distributors.

If you don't have a local theatrical supply house, don't forget to check shops that cater to dancers. They often carry a basic supply of theatrical makeup, too. Your local grocery store is also an excellent source for some of the materials used here, such as gelatin, pectin, food coloring, and the like.

Even if you prefer to order your supplies by mail, over the phone, or through the Internet, it's always good to have a local shop to go to when you suddenly discover you've used your last stipple sponge or need a small bottle of effects gel.

The following appendix provides ample room for you to make note of any local suppliers you have and any additional discoveries you made in the process of working your way through this book.

Appendix C: Notes

This section is provided for you to use as you see fit—jotting down notes on makeup, documenting research, doodling while you're waiting for a bus, and so on. It's pretty much just a couple of blank pages, after all.

However, you'll also find a pair of illustrations to help you in your own makeup designs. You'll find a front and profile head sketch, which you can use to plan out your own makeup designs. Feel free to photocopy them from the book for your personal use.

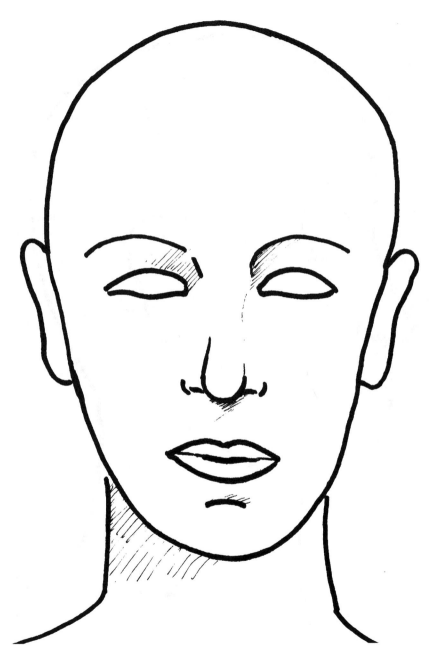

Figure C.1   Full-face model to help you do your own concept sketches and makeup plots.

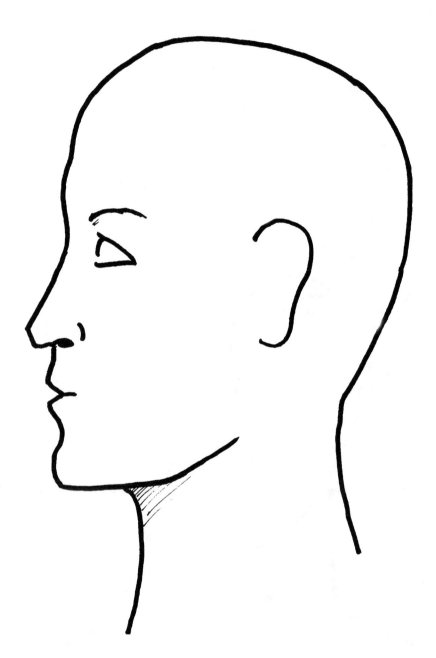

Figure C.2   A profile face for side-view sketches and makeup plots.

Notes

Notes

Notes

Notes

Notes

Notes

Notes

Notes

About the CD

The attached CD contains a multitude of information and resources for you, including

- ➲ full-color versions of the step-by-step photographs for each makeup design demonstrated in the book
- ➲ printable versions of the shadow reference and full-face and profile makeup design blanks
- ➲ a list of suppliers, with clickable hotlinks to the websites of FX makeup supply manufacturers and retailers

System Requirements

Windows/PC	**Macintosh**
Pentium Processor (233Mhz or higher)	PowerPC Processor
Windows 95 (or higher)	System 8 (or higher)
64 MB RAM (more recommended)	64 MB RAM (more recommended)
SVGA Color Display (or better)	SVGA Color Display (or better)
8x CD-ROM Drive (or faster)	8x CD-ROM Drive (or faster)
QuickTime 4.0 (or higher)	QuickTime 4.0 (or higher)